Echoes of Gita

OrangeBooks Publication

1st Floor, Rajhans Arcade, Mall Road, Kohka, Bhilai, Chhattisgarh 490020
Website: **www.orangebooks.in**

First Edition, 2025

ISBN: 978-93-6554-393-3

Price: Rs. 300.00

Printed in India

Echoes of Gita

धर्मसंस्थापनार्थाय सम्भवामि युगे युगे

Lakshmi Narasimha Diwakar Addala

OrangeBooks Publication

www.orangebooks.in

Preface

Since childhood, I have been inspired by the great stories of the Mahabharata and Ramayana. I admired every heroic character and strongly trusted the Supreme Power. Understanding these epics teaches many lessons.

This manuscript presents my interpretation of the Bhagavad Gita. Rather than word-to-word translation of every verse it emphasises the essential teachings that Krishna imparted to humanity through Arjuna.

The Bhagavad Gita begins with the word Dharma (Righteousness), providing valuable insights into leading a meaningful life. This conversation, which takes place between Krishna (Narayana) and Arjuna (Nara) in the backdrop of the Mahabharata War, delves into the nuances of 'the Right and the Wrong' and ways of living.

These principles of Sanatana Dharma (eternal righteousness) apply to the entire Humankind and do not belong to any ethnicity. Adhering to moral values is everyone's responsibility. Sadly, Sanatana Dharma is misinterpreted and considered to be associated only with Hinduism.

Before the Kurukshetra war, the Pandavas and the Kauravas encountered numerous conflicts, frequently engaged in intense dialogues, and challenged each other to execute one another. However, at the crucial moment,

Arjuna found himself in emotional trauma. He was confused about whether to fight against his family members, such as uncles, cousins, and respected gurus or to stop the war and save their lives. Arjuna surrendered to grief, reflecting the vulnerabilities of any ordinary human being.

It can be observed that Krishna does not counter Arjuna until he completely expresses his thoughts and requests that Krishna decide on the course of action.

Common communication errors include failing to pay attention or jumping to conclusions without listening to or understanding the problem statement. People often justify their stand or perspective based on the facts available in their capacity without having a comprehensive view, leading to communication gaps or misjudgement.

To succeed, one should practice active listening and communication skills, seek guidance, and avoid preoccupied thoughts.

Krishna listened carefully to Arjuna before HE started most precious teachings (GITA).

As mentioned in the Bhagavata Puran or Mahabharata, Krishna lived by example throughout his life, undertaking every task with integrity and virtue (righteousness).

He fought against every obstacle or demonic person to uphold Justice. At the same time, to his mother, He was a mischievous boy, to his friends, a playful companion, to his beloved, he was a romantic boy, and to those in need, a loyal friend. A King Maker protecting his people and diligently performed his day-to-day Sanatana Dharma rituals like any ordinary human being. Krishna emphasised if he did not adhere to Dharma, no one would. Protecting the Sanatana Dharma was his foremost priority.

Practice before you preach. Be a torch bearer.

The verses of the Bhagavad Gita are perfectly placed and sequenced. I will highlight them as needed. As mentioned earlier, this book is not a word-for-word translation of the Bhagavad Gita, and I do not intend to do so. However, I will share insights into the Gita and some teachings around interpersonal, communication, leadership skills, and, most importantly, 'ways of living'.

The Bhagavad Gita conversation opens with the words ‘Dharma Kshetre’. The word Dharma, right from the beginning, conveys great significance. There are no higher principles in human actions than Dharma. And the word Kshetre means the physical body. Perform righteous actions with the help of physical body to lead a meaningful life.

I offer my respects to the great Gurus who imparted their immense knowledge and shared their insights on various Vedas to Humankind. In my opinion, they are the true sons of Goddess Saraswati. While I was curious in understanding History (Itihasas), their teachings had an invaluable impact on me, guiding me to think beyond and look at these Puranas from a different perspective.

Many people may assume Bhagavat Gita is very complex, difficult to understand and maybe something to learn or comprehend after retirement because of which, people tend to ignore or stay away. This book is an attempt to eliminate such illusions and generate curiosity to learn full version of the Bhagavat Gita and enlighten oneself.

I beg pardon if I have made any mistakes.

Lakshmi Narasimha Diwakar. Addala

The Backdrop

Upon the request of Dhritarastra, Sanjaya, with his divine eyes, visualises the battlefield and narrates the happenings of the Kurukshetra (the land where the great Mahabharata War happened). As he gazes upon the battlefield from Hastinapur Palace (current New Delhi), Sanjaya observes Duryodhana approaching his Guru Drona (who is strategising the war on behalf of Kuru dynasty), and assess the battlefield and speaking the following.

One might wonder how Sanjaya is able to observe the events on the battlefield from a distance. Background – Vedavyasa (The Sage), foreseeing the future, blesses Sanjaya with a divine eye to witness the happening at the Mahabharat Battlefield and relay minute-to-minute happenings to Dhritarashtra. Imagine today's satellites transmitting digital content in real-time on televisions, phones, live video calls, etc. After understanding the Vedas, Indian scriptures or architectural marvels, it is quite evident that it was a very advanced civilisation about 5000+ years ago.

Contents

Chapter 1

Arjuna Vishadayogam (Mind's Emotional Trauma)

धर्मक्षेत्रे कुरुक्षेत्रे समवेता युयुत्सवः ।

मामकाः पाण्डवाश्चैव किमकुर्वत सञ्जय ॥

Dharmakshetre Kurukshetre Samaetaa Yuyutsavaha

Maamakaaha Paandavaaschiva Kima Kurvata Sanjaya.

In the first verse, Dhritarastra asks Sanjaya by using "our people" and "Pandavas". Dhritarastra always took the side of his son even though he knew that his son is not legally inheriting or capable of inheriting the property or the kingdom and fighting against his own brother's sons. However, I believe that Dhritarastra being a scholar in Vedic sciences, he inadvertently uttered the word "Dharma" to start his conversation and learn about the happenings of the Kurukshetra War.

Sanjaya starts narrating as Duryodhana speaks to Guru Dronacharya. The first few verses demonstrate Duryodhana's competence in pleasing people and gaining loyalty.

पश्यैतां पाण्डुपुत्राणामाचार्य महतीं चमूम्।

व्यूढां द्रुपदपुत्रेण तव शिष्येण धीमता ॥

Pashyetaam Paanduputraanaam Aacharya
Mahateem Chamoom

Vyudhaam Drupadaputrena Tava Sishyena Dheemataa

He requests his teacher, Dronacharya, to examine the strategic arrangements of the battlefield organised by Drupadaputra (Son of Drupada - Drustadyumn) for the Pandavas.

Dhuryodana knows the history and the ego conflicts between Drupada (father of Drustradyumn) and Drona. How two great friends became lifetime enemies. Previously, Drona won a few battles occurred due to their personal ego clashes against Drupada. Subsequently, Drupada performed an immense Yagna (worship) to have a boon to bless him with a son who can kill Drona, thus giving birth to "Dristadyumn". By mentioning Dristadyumn to start with, Duryodhana is refreshing his Guru's memories of past rivalries and provoking his Guru's anger and ego.

भवान्भीष्मश्च कर्णश्च कृपश्च समितिञ्जयः।

अश्वत्थामा विकर्णश्च सौमदत्तिस्तथैव च ॥

Bhavaan Beemascha Karnascha Krupascha Samitinjayaha
Aswadhaamaa Vikarnascha Somadatthistathaiva Cha

After assessing the battlefield of the rivals (Pandavas), Duryodhana also reminds him of the great warriors from the Kuru army that Drona is heading and strategising the battlefield. He starts with "Yourselves (Bhavan)" and refers to Dronacharya first.

Here, he refers to Drona as a mighty warrior and addresses his name before Bheeshma (the grandfather) or his kin to emotionally secure his loyalty towards him. He then sequentially goes to Bheeshma, the senior most and oldest well-wisher of the Kuru dynasty, followed by his best friend Karna and others.

The sequence of the names Duryodhana addresses demonstrates his ability to emotionally influence people's minds to gain their loyalty and compel them to fight for him without any biases towards the Pandavas (Drona's beloved disciples).

It is crucial to use the right words at the right time. It is always better to be aware of the surroundings and possible challenges ahead. Assess the audience, their strengths for a fruitful conversation and, simultaneously, possess self-awareness to manage the situation. Duryodhana is exhibiting leadership and administrative skills. However, his skills are utilised for selfish goals and following the demonic nature.

धर्मसंस्थापनार्थाय सम्भवामि युगे युगे

The path of righteousness is a very tough and long journey. However, the peace of Mind and satisfaction after achieving the desired results provide eternal happiness.

To please and encourage Duryodhana, Bheeshma, Drona, and others from the Kuru side blew their conches to send the message to the Pandavas that they were ready for the war.

As a response, Pandavas also blew their conches.

पाञ्चजन्यं हृषीकेशो देवदत्तं धनञ्जयः ।
पौण्ड्रं दध्मौ महाशङ्खं भीमकर्मा वृकोदरः ॥

Panchajanyam Hrushikesho Devadattam Dhananjayaha
Poundram Dadhmou Mahaashankham Bheemakarmaa Vrukodaraha

It is essential to understand the sequence of the conches' sounds here. The first sound came from Krishan's Panchajanya, followed by Arjuna's Devadattam.

According to the Itihasas (history), Panchajanya is the conch associated to Lord Vishnu. By mentioning that Krishna blew Panchajanya, the Vedas identify HIM as the incarnation of Lord Vishnu, who descended to earth to eliminate the demonic people, reduce the burden from Mother Earth, and restore Dharma.

अर्जुन उवाच ।

सेनयोरुभयोर्मध्ये रथं स्थापय मेऽच्युत

Arjuna Uvacha

Senayorubhayor Madhye Ratham Sthaapayame Achyuta

Arjuna first wanted to assess his surroundings and sought to evaluate the strengths and weaknesses of his opposition (enemies). Without hesitation, he requested Krishna to position the chariot in the middle of the battlefield to observe the vast army assembled before him, ready for the battle.

भीष्मद्रोणप्रमुखतः सर्वेषां च महीक्षिताम् ।

उवाच पार्थ पश्यैतान्समवेतान्कुरूनिति ॥

Bheeshmadronapramukhataha Sarveshaam Cha Maheekshitaam

Uvaacha Partha Pashyetaansamavetaan Kuruniti

As Arjuna observed the opposition, instead of assessing the army and their powers like Duryodhana, all that he could observe in front of him was his most beloved Grandfather (Bheeshma), Teacher (Guru Drona),

Brothers, Sons, Children, Grandchildren, Friends and NOT the enemies.

The sequence of names is also different from what Duryodhana observed. Arjuna doesn't have to please anyone. He is looking at his most beloved Grandfather, Bheeshma, first, then his Guru Drona, followed by others.

This is a widespread dilemma for any normal human being when people have a conflicting situation within their family and friends. They often face 'Dharma Sandeham' (a dilemma between emotions and righteousness) to fight or argue against beloved people to prove a point of view. As per Sanatana Dharma, righteousness must prevail irrespective of the family or the friend.

Bhagavad Gita is a guide for all those who are in conflicting situations within close connects, families, friends, colleagues, or near and dear. It guides them to make the right decisions, especially when fighting for righteousness over self-esteem, selfishness, and demonic goals. Since Arjuna's grieves are common struggles of humankind, it can be considered as Arjuna representing Humankind and asked a series of questions to Krishna.

As we go deep into the context, the Bhagavat Gita not only teaches how to handle conflicting situations but also how to lead a happy and healthy life.

दृष्ट्वेमं स्वजनं कृष्ण युयुत्सुं समुपस्थितम्

सीदन्ति मम गात्राणि मुखं च परिशुष्यति ।

वेपथुश्च शरीरे मे रोमहर्षश्च जायते ॥

Drustvemam Swajanam Krishna Yuyutsum Samupasthitam

Seedanti Mama Gaatraani Mukham Cha Parishushyati

Vepayuscha Sareere Me Romaharshascha Jaayate

Observing his own family (swajanam) and friends eagerly waiting to kill each other to win the war to benefit one demonic, self-esteemed, selfish leader (Dhuryodana), Arjuna was caught in a dilemma. He was overwhelmed imagining the result of the war.

This posed numerous questions in his Mind. The expected result of the war for Pandavas, is to win and establish righteousness, justice, provide unbiased leadership, work towards the prosperity of the people, and have a happy life with families and friends. However, Arjuna could foresee killing thousands of people for whom this battle was fought for. When these families, friends and people are executed, what will he and his family be doing by owning such a kingdom and ruling it? He felt it would be better option to get killed and leave the kingdom to Duryodhana instead of killing his kin and kith.

For quick reference: The size of the army assembled at The Kurukshetra.

There are 11 Akshohinis from the side of Kuru and 7 Akshohinis from Pandava, forming a total of 18 Akshohinis. Arjuna could only visualise the death of millions of people and an ocean of blood.

Count	Group Name	Chariots	Solders	Horses	Elephants	Total
	One Sena	1	5	3	1	10
3*Sena	Patti	3	15	9	3	30
3*Patti	Gulma	9	45	27	9	90
3*Gulma	Gana	27	135	81	27	270
3*Gana	Vahini	81	405	243	81	810
3*Vahini	Pritana	243	1215	729	243	2430
3*Pritana	Chamu	729	3645	2187	729	7290
3*Chamu	Anikuni	2187	10935	6561	2187	21870
10* Anikuni	Akshohini	21870	109350	65610	21870	218700

7 Akshohinis of Pandava Army

Count	Group Name	Chariots	Solders	Horses	Elephants	Total
7* Akshohini		153090	765459	459270	153090	1530900

11 Akshohinis of Kuru Army

Count	Group Name	Chariott	Solders	Horses	Elephants	Total
11* Akshohini		240570	1202850	721710	240570	2405700

Total 39,36,600.

He sensed a section of races and classes of families would be executed by the end of the war. Many young girls will become widows. As the sects are eliminated, there will be interracial, class and caste marriages. This will result in mixed ethnicities; the children born to those will not be able to identify themselves by a specific ethnicity. This will eventually impact traditional rituals such as Pitru Karma (the rituals performed for the deceased forefathers for their peaceful transition to the heavenly abode). If the Pitru Karma is not performed, the deceased will not be able to attain Moksh (Eternal Peace). Arjuna's foresight of the war was nothing but destruction, and he does not see any positive outcome.

अहो बत महत्पापं कर्तुं व्यवसिता वयम् ।
यद्राज्यसुखलोभेन हन्तुं स्वजनमुद्यताः ॥

Aho Bata Mahatpaapam Kartum Vyavastitaa Vayam
Yatraajyasukhalobhena Hantum Swajanamudhyataaha

He says, 'Oh Krishna, unknowingly, WE came here to commit such a huge crime and destruction'. I am okay to get killed by these people and give away the kingdom; instead of fighting this battle and be the reason for destruction and Adharma.

Interestingly, Arjuna also includes Krishna in this conversation and says, 'WE' are here to commit such a colossal crime. The war is fought for the rights of the Pandavas, not for Krishna.

You own your career or destiny. No one will come for your rescue; it is better you fight your own battles. It's a fight between the Pandavas and the Kauravas. Arjuna is fighting for his rights.

As a matter of fact, Krishna and his kingdom (Mathura) was attacked by enemies several times in the past, with an army of about one Akshouhini each time. Krishna and Balarama (Brother of Krishna) fought those battles all alone, protecting their people and land. When Jarasandha tasked Kalayavana to attack Mathura (birth place of Krishna), Krishna instructed Viswavakarma (The architect of Gods) to build a village, 'Dwaraka', overnight in the middle of the ocean to protect his people. This submerged village can be seen even today near Gujarat. Krishna alone got Kalayavana killed with his war tactics.

If Krishna wanted to fight the Kurukshetra battle, it would not have taken him much time to finish. However, Krishna chose not to touch any weapon during the Kurukshetra war but let the Pandavas fight their own battle.

As a leader, Krishna let his team fight their battle (execute the given task) while providing relevant and appropriate guidance from time-to-time to make them successful. Leaders should always encourage and help their team achieve their success instead of discouraging and taking over the task to complete by themselves. Krishna was there throughout the war for the Pandavas, guiding them and playing the role of a great leader/mentor. On the other hand, it is equally important to trust your leader and follow the guidance to achieve the best results.

Had Krishna fought the war, then only Krishna would have been remembered, and the great warriors like Arjuna, Bheema, and many others would have been erased from the books of history. Credit is given to the great warriors who fought for righteousness and ultimately established Justice.

Saying so, with a heavy heart and eyes full of tears, Arjuna drops his mighty bow, 'Gandivam' in deep sorrow.

Chapter 2

Sankhya Yogam (Essence of Birth and Death)

तं तथा कृपयाविष्टमश्रुपूर्णाकुलेक्षणम् ।
विषीदन्तमिदं वाक्यमुवाच मधुसूदनः ॥

Tam Tatha Krupayaavishtum Asrupurnakulekshanam
Visheedantamidam Vaakyamuvaacha Madhusudanaha

Sanjaya continues to narrate—after listening to Arjuna grief, Madhusudhana speaks as below.

श्रीभगवानुवाच ।
कुतस्त्वा कश्मलमिदं विषमे समुपस्थितम् ।
अनार्यजुष्टमस्वर्ग्यमकीर्तिकरमर्जुन ॥

Bhagavan Uvacha

Kutastvaa Kashmalamidam Vishame Samupasthitam

Anaryajustam Aswargyam Akeertikaram Arjuna

The Bhagavad Gita consistently refers to Krishna as the Supreme God, hence the word Sri Bhagavan Uvacha (The Supreme God Spoke).

Without hesitation or empathy, Krishna comes straight to the point and challenges Arjuna. Where did he get this venomous and unruly thought which will not lead him to the heavens or will give him any glory? For Krishna, anything which is Adharma (wickedness, evil or immorality) should not exist. He descended from heavenly abode to earth only to eradicate the demons and establish and uphold Humankind with the laws of nature (Dharma).

क्लैब्यं मा स्म गमः पार्थ नैतत्त्वय्युपपद्यते ।

क्षुद्रं हृदयदौर्बल्यं त्यक्त्वोत्तिष्ठ परन्तप ॥

Kleybyam Maa Sma Gamaha Paartha Naitatvayyupapadyate

Kshudram Hrudayadourbalyam Tyaktvetthishtha Parantapa

Krishna refers Arjuna as Parantapa in this verse. Krishna always observed Arjuna as determined, brave, and willing to fight for Justice, hence the word 'Parantapa'. He is puzzled how such a warrior became weak-minded and faint hearted at this crucial moment.

It is essential to remain courageous and stand firm to principles when facing tough challenges. Surrendering to fears or emotional trauma will never result in success. Hence, Krishna challenges Arjuna to explain how he can be so weak at a crucial moment, such as the magnitude of the Mahabharata War.

It is crucial to offer constructive and timely feedback. If the manager tries to be empathetic and avoids providing constructive feedback, the key message or significance of the feedback is lost. This can cause incorrect decision-making and may have a long-lasting impact on the feedback receiver's personal growth or on the initiatives they are assigned to.

A structured and firm feedback is very important at every stage of life between parents, children, friends, teachers and students, mentors and mentees.

It is always better to look at the big picture or end-to-end view. Those who are siloed will not be able to understand the big picture and operate for a more significant cause. It is essential as a leadership behaviour to provide timely feedback to mitigate foreseeable issues.

People often face emotional dilemmas during tough conversations or decisions involving loved ones, friends, or colleagues. While trying to be empathetic and spare others' feelings, people may take on unnecessary blame or pain, leading to self-destruction, reduced confidence, and poor decision-making.

कथं भीष्ममहं सङ्ख्ये द्रोणं च मधुसूदन ।
इषुभिः प्रतियोत्स्यामि पूजार्हावरिसूदन ॥

Katham Bheeshamamaham Sankhye Dronam Cha Madhusudana
Ishubhihi Pratiyotsyaami Poojarhaavarisudana

गुरूनहत्वा हि महानुभावान्
श्रेयो भोक्तुं भैक्ष्यमपीह लोके ।
हत्वार्थकामांस्तु गुरूनिहैव
भुञ्जीय भोगान् रुधिरप्रदिग्धान् ॥

Jurunahatvaa Hi Mahaanubhaavaan
Sreyo Bhokthum Bhokshamapeeha Loke
Katvaarthamaamaamstu Guroonihaiva
Bhujeeya Bhogaan Rudhirapradigdhaan

Arjuna is referring to Krishna as Madhusudhana. Krishna has many names attributed to him. Why referring Krishna as Madhusudana in this verse?

Madhu is the name of the Demon, and Sudhana means killer. Referring to him as 'O Killer of Madhu'. If we go back to history, at the beginning of the universe, when Lord Vishnu was in a state of conscious sleep (Yoga Nidra), a wax fell out of his ear, creating two most powerful Demons named Madhu and Kaitabha. The very first demons of the universe. Both demons started destroying the universe and Mother Earth. Mahavishnu fought for 1000s of years and finally managed to kill them to protect the universe. Since he killed Madhu and Kaitabha, he is referred to as Madhukaitabhare (Madhu+Kaitabha+Hara (killer)) and Madhusudhana.

In my observation, Krishna is going to destroy misconceptions and unnecessary and unwarranted attachments that Arjuna is associated with, hence referring to him as Madhusudhana.

With tears in his eyes, Arjuna says, “Oh, Madhusudhana, they are my own Bheeshma, my revered grandfather and Drona, my beloved teacher”.

It is evident how emotionally Arjuna was traumatised, thinking that he would have to kill his beloved grandfather, guru and many others to achieve victory.

Arjuna also substantiates his statements with examples such as killing the teacher (Guru) is an irreversible sin and cannot kill him for materialistic bliss. As an alternative, he would instead get killed by them or live in poverty.

As per Sanatana Dharma, some sins are considered the most devastating, one among them is killing the Guru.

Removing Gurus disrupts the chain of passing wisdom to future generations. Imagine a world without teachers.

कार्पण्यदोषोपहतस्वभावः
पृच्छामि त्वां धर्मसम्मूढचेताः।
यच्छ्रेयः स्यान्निश्चितं ब्रूहि तन्मे
शिष्यस्तेऽहं शाधि मां त्वां प्रपन्नम् ॥

Karpanyadoshopahataswabhaavaha
Pruchchaami Tvaam Dharmasammudhachetaaha
Ychchreyaha Syaannischitam Bruhi Tanme
Sishyasteham Saadhi Maam Tvaam Prapannam

Arjuna continues – 'People will refer to me as a selfish person if I kill them for the sake of materialistic happiness'.

After explaining his thought process and letting out his grief, Arjuna finally requests Krishna to consider him HIS disciple and instruct him firmly on his duty.

Now that Arjuna surrenders to the lotus feet of Krishna and requests him to instruct his course of action, Krishna starts his teachings to enlighten Arjuna (Humankind irrespective of region or religion) and show the path towards Moksha (Eternal peace/happiness). If one disconnects from the outcomes of action (attachments), no pain can touch them.

श्रीभगवानुवाच ।

अशोच्यानन्वशोचस्त्वं प्रज्ञावादांश्च भाषसे ।

गतासूनगतासूंश्च नानुशोचन्ति पण्डिताः॥

Bhagavan Uvacha

Asouchyaanavasouchastvam Pragyavaadamscha Bhaashase

Jataasunagataasumscha Naanusouchati Panditaaha

Krishna wittingly says, "You are making worthless statements while speaking like a wise man with the context of legitimate examples (that Arjuna considered). You are sobbing for something that doesn't require to be. The people around you — they all were there before us; they're here and will be thereafter. "In this chapter, Krishna establishes the cycle of life and the concept of rebirth.

Sanatana Dharma strongly trusts in the concept of rebirth. He relates death and rebirth to the transformation from an infant to childhood to an adolescent to an older adult. Just because one grows to the next stage of life, they are not worried about yesteryears. Just like people change their clothes, the Soul migrates to the new body as the current one ceases to exist one day. It can also be referred to as the caterpillar leaves the leaf that it is crawling only after connecting to the new one.

The Soul is the ultimate truth. Even if someone believes the physical body is everything, it must cease to exist one day. All material objects have a starting and an ending point. Brave and educated people will not worry about such interim happiness. Treasure the imperishable—'The Soul'.

People are generally attached and obsessed with materialistic objects such as the properties, the work we do, the people we live with or the company we work with. When we observe with a different lens, all of these will cease to exist one day. Over a period, people tend to forget the past and move on. Everything in this material world is perishable and is interim whether happiness or sadness.

Krishna implies such happiness and sadness to the ever-changing climatic conditions.

मात्रास्पर्शास्तु कौन्तेय शीतोष्णसुखदुःखदाः ।
आगमापायिनोऽनित्यास्तांस्तितिक्षस्व भारत ॥

Maatrasparsaastu Kaunteya Seetoshna Sukhadukhadaaha
Aagamaapaayinonityaastaam Stitikshasva Bhaarata

All material joy and miseries are like summer and winter or hot and cold. They are experiences of human consciousness. They will come and go and are not here to stay forever. We feel happy for our achievements and sad for our losses. As time goes by, they too will fadeaway.

It is essential to know the long-term goal, or eternal happiness, instead of temporary ones.

वासांसि जीर्णानि यथा विहाय

नवानि गृह्णाति नरोऽपराणि ।

तथा शरीराणि विहाय जीर्णा-

न्यन्यानि संयाति नवानि देही ॥

Vaasaamsi Jeernani Yathaa Vihaya
Navaani Gruhnaati Naroparaani
Tatha Sareerani Vihaaya Jeernaani
Anyaani Samyaati Navaani Dehi

The Soul has no birth or death. The Soul cannot kill or get killed by someone. It cannot be set on fire, drenched with water, or blown away by air. It cannot be destroyed, burnt, or drowned. It is forever (Sanatani) and is everywhere.

जातस्य हि ध्रुवो मृत्युर्ध्रुवं जन्म मृतस्य च ।

तस्मादपरिहार्येऽर्थे न त्वं शोचितुमर्हसि ॥

Jaatastya Hi Dhruvo Mrutyurdhruvam
Janma Mrutasya Cha
Tasmaadaparihaaryerthe Na Tvam Sochitumarhasi

The death or end is inevitable. Why worry about something that is not going to last forever? In other words, worry about something that lasts forever. The enlightened and wise people do not worry about such temporary problems. 'So, get up and do your duty. Fight and win the war.

Krishna, in this chapter, established that the existence of Soul is forever.

In simple terms, a new toy excites the child and bring happiness and sad when it perishes. The child cries for a while before eventually forgetting about it. As adults, parents understand it is a temporary loss for him and don't cry with the kid because they know the toy is perishable. Like warm or cold weather, sadness or happiness will come and go.

कर्मण्येवाधिकारस्ते मा फलेषु कदाचन ।
मा कर्मफलहेतुर्भूर्मा ते सङ्गोऽस्त्वकर्मणि ॥

Karmanyevaadhikaaraste Maa Phaleshu Kadaachana
Maa Karmaphalaheturbhurmaa Te Sangstvakarmani

Krishna instructs Arjuna to face the war and perform his duty as a warrior. If he escapes, generations will remember him as a fugitive. It is more insulting for a great warrior than death.

The worst result of the war could be that Arjuna might get killed. However, in the end, people will remember him as a great warrior, and he attained a heavenly abode because he fought for Dharma.

Coincidentally, Arjuna has got such a great opportunity.

In my opinion, taking the right decisions with determination and fearlessness is essential. Running away from challenging situations will not make people stronger and create opportunities. Apprehensions are the interim fears of life. If the decisions are correct and the cause of righteousness, one should not be worried or afraid of the consequences. One should always stand with Dharma.

Dharma is a relative term and cannot be misinterpreted with Justice. Justice may be an outcome of the deeds of righteousness. What is right for you may not be right for the other person. However, Dharma remains steadfast and eternal.

The essence of this chapter is that Krishna suggests Arjuna get enlightened and rise above this interim happiness or anguish and mature like a Saint (Shitapragyna) who is not attached to any of the duties.

अर्जुन उवाच ।
स्थितप्रज्ञस्य का भाषा समाधिस्थस्य केशव ।
स्थितधीः किं प्रभाषेत किमासीत व्रजेत किम् ॥

Arjuna Uvacha
Sthitapragnya Kaa Bhaashaa Samaadhisthasya Kesava
Sthiradheehi Kim Prabhaasheta Kimaaseeta Vrajeta Kim

Arjuna gets involved in the conversation and started enquiring more into the Brahma Gyana (divine wisdom) and wants to understand how a Saint (Sthitapragnya) look like, their walk, behaviour and how they represent themselves.

Krishna explains, 'One becomes a Saint when they are not attached to the outcome of their duties. They are not attached to the Triguna (Satva, Rajo, Tamo gunas) and rise above them.

Satva Guna represents being Simple and Peaceful.

Rajo Guna represents Passion, Love and Lust.

Finally, Tamo Guna represents Anger, Destruction, etc.

Every duty performed is attached to one of the Trigunas (Satvarajastamo gunas). When one exercises duties with a detachment to the Trigunas (Tri–Three) and leaves, the dual facet emotions such as Happy or Sad, Win or Lose,

Love or Hate and many more will become the Saint (Sthitapragnya).

The Mind's nature is wavering, and it tries to get emotional and attached to the Trigunas (Satvarajastamo gunas). Krishna indicates that one should rise beyond Triguna.

If we observe the fundamentals, Arjuna's concerns are very appropriate. Killing teachers and a vast army will only lead to destruction. However, who is Arjuna instructed to kill? Those who are following injustice, possessing demonic characteristics, and or supporting and fighting for Adharm. Does it mean that we (common people) are recommended to massacre others? Do we have right to do so? No.

In this context, we should interpret the message to kill the unruly thoughts in our minds that can cause self-destruction and harm others.

Chapter 3

Karma Yoga (Essence of Work without attachment to desire)

अर्जुन उवाच ।

ज्यायसी चेत्कर्मणस्ते मता बुद्धिर्जनार्दन ।

तत्किं कर्मणि घोरे मां नियोजयसि केशव ॥

Arjuna Uvacha

Jyayaseechetkarmanasyte mataa budhri janardhana

tat kim karmani ghore maam niyojayasi kesava

व्यामिश्रेणेव वाक्येन बुद्धिं मोहयसीव मे ।

तदेकं वद निश्चित्य येन श्रेयोऽहमाप्नुयाम् ॥

Vyamisreneva vaakyena budhim mohayaseeva me

Tadekam vada nishchitya sreyho ahamatpnuyaam

In the previous chapter (Sankhya Yogam), Krishna advocated that one needs to possess characteristics of a Saint to attain Moksha. At the same time, he suggested that Arjuna perform his duty and fight the battle. Confused and doubtful, Arjuna requested Krishna clarify and suggest a definitive course of action.

Executing materialistic duties will continue to bind the Humankind to the circle of life. Then why one should perform materialistic duties when the goal is to attain Moksha through Saintly (Sthitapragya) qualities? One can excuse oneself from all duties and try to become the Saint.

Knowledge will always deepen as one tries to inquire and have a two-way conversation rather than accepting everything that is told. The Bhagavad Gita or any other Asthadasa Puranas (18 Puranas—Vedic scriptures) are about seeking knowledge about various topics. Hence they all are documented in the form of Prashna and Uttar (Question and Answer)

श्रीभगवानुवाच

लोकेऽस्मिन् द्विविधा निष्ठा पुरा प्रोक्ता मयानघ ।

ज्ञानयोगेन साङ्ख्यानां कर्मयोगेन योगिनाम् ॥

Sri Bhagavan Uvacha

Loke Asmin Dwividhaa Nishthapura Proktaa Mayaanagha

Gyaanayogena Saankhyanaam Karmayogena Yoginaam

न कर्मणामनारम्भान्नैष्कर्म्यं पुरुषोऽश्नुते ।

न च संन्यसनादेव सिद्धिं समधिगच्छति ॥

Na Karmanam Aarambhaanaishkarmayam Purushyonsrute

Na Cha Samnyasanaadeva Sidhim Samadhigachati

There are two ways to attain Moksha: living like a saint and realising the Soul and performing duties with Dharma (righteousness).

It is not possible to live without discharging such actions. One must perform daily responsibilities and rituals to survive.

नियतं कुरु कर्म त्वं कर्म ज्यायो ह्यकर्मणः ।

शरीरयात्रापि च ते न प्रसिद्ध्येदकर्मणः ॥

Niyaram Kuru Karma Tvam Karma Jyaaye
Hyukarmanaha
Sareerayaatraapi Cha Te Na Prasidhdhayodakarmanaha

As living beings are attached to the material senses, they perform their duties with or without their will and wish. However, while executing their duties, one should control their desires and senses.

Humankind lives and evolves through consuming food and gain energies to perform Yagnas. Performing ritual sacrifices (yagna) causes environmental changes. Such changes will lead to rain, which helps grow food.

If we closely observe, Krishna is explaining the process of Kharif about 5000+ years ago. The education is not just about ways of living but also about how nature operates.

At the beginning of the universe, along with Humankind's creation, Vedic literature was also scripted. I consider these Vedic Scriptures as a 'Guide' for the humankind. The ancient people lived by performing Yagna (ritual sacrifices offered into the consecrated fire). Chanting Vedas and offering ritual sacrifices (Samidha) into the sacred fire which served as a communication channel to the divine gods. The universe comprehends the 'sounds' produced while chanting the Vedas. The mixture of the sounds and the environmental changes caused by the Yagna are the messages to the Heavenly Gods to bestow their blessings to the Humankind. These rituals were conducted for the wealth and prosperity both individuals and and the Humankind.

Consider it a satellite channel in modern life. No physical wires connect our digital devices to the satellite and the receivers. Similarly, the sounds emerged while chanting these Vedas act as a communication channel between Humankind and supernatural powers.

The Sanatana Dharma always advocated for helping and sharing with each other. Those who attain wealth and prosperity and do not perform sacrifices are considered robbers as they do not help maintain the balance of nature. It is taking pleasure from nature without giving anything back in return.

Krishna (Sanatana Dharma) advocates the value of giving. While performing duties to fulfil desires, it is equally important to offer in return.

In my opinion, Indian festivals emphasise the importance of sharing. The offerings are given to consecrated fire, old clothes to people in need, sharing and gifting to families, friends and people in need during special occasions, offerings (Dakshinas) to the Brahmins and many more. The wealth was to be distributed and not to be kept with oneself. Offering Dakshina(donation) to the Brahmans will sustain and establish 'Vedas' education. Without Dakshina, the Brahmins who are in the field of Sanatana Dharma and play the roles of priest, struggle to survives which will force them to choose other fields for their living. That eventually hinder the spreading of Vedic knowledge. Thanking the labourer, farmers, gurus, rishis, and the divine gods is essential and keeps the people grounded.

Imagine the passing of education or wealth as a Dominic chain reaction. If we remove one Domino, the chain reaction will stop and will not move forward. So, be Dominic in the entire chain reaction and help continue the process of nature.

अर्जुन उवाच ।

अथ केन प्रयुक्तोऽयं पापं चरति पूरुषः ।

अनिच्छन्नपि वार्ष्णेय बलादिव नियोजितः ॥

Arjuna Uvacha

Atha Ken Prayukthoyam paapam charati poorushaha

Anichinnapi vaarshneya balaadiva niyojitaha

Arjuna asks, "Why are people willingly or unwillingly performing sins? What are the influencing factors for doing so?"

This question is very relevant to everyone's day-to-day life. People knowingly or unknowingly perform many sins. Understanding the influencing factors and acting accordingly with awareness and a sense of responsibility is important.

श्रीभगवानुवाच ।

काम एष क्रोध एष रजोगुणसमुद्भवः ।

महाशनो महापाप्मा विद्ध्येनमिह वैरिणम् ॥

Bhagavan Uvacha

Kaama Esha Krodha Esha Rajogunasamudbhavaha

Mahaasano Mahaapaapmaa Vidhyayenamiha Vairinam

Krishna firmly states that Desire, Lust, and Anger are key influencing factors that control Humankind's senses and cause them to perform sins.

इन्द्रियाणि पराण्याहुरिन्द्रियेभ्यः परं मनः ।

मनसस्तु परा बुद्धिर्यो बुद्धेः परतस्तु सः ॥

Indriyaani Paraanyaahuhu Indriyebhyaha Param Manaha

Manasastu paraa Budhdhiryo Budhdheha Paratastu Saha

He further elaborates – 'Senses are more potent than the human being. The Mind is more powerful than the senses, and the Soul is more powerful than the Mind. Desire, Lust and Anger control these senses. It is only the Soul which is not attached to any of the worldly desires.

Each living being possesses eleven elements that influence their life: five physical, five senses and one Mind.

Physical—The eyes, nose, tongue, ear, and skin are more powerful than human beings as they directly control the senses that are related to them. They are powerful over the physical body as they are the key elements for one to perform duty.

Senses - Vision, Smell, Taste, Hearing and Touch. They are more potent than the physical elements as they influence them to fulfil their desires.

The Mind is even more powerful than these 10 elements, which instruct living beings to fulfil their desires as they are attached to emotions, desires, likes, and dislikes. All of these emotions have an end-of-life.

The Soul is not connected to any of these. As established in the previous chapter, the Soul can never be touched, lit to fire, drenched or drowned.

Intellectuals are fully aware that the Soul is indestructible and invincible. Such a person will never be attached to the emotions or senses which have an end of life.

For ages, people who follow Sanatana Dharma are recommended to perform Ekadasi Upavasam (By controlling desires and lust that influence the eleven senses and devote the day contemplating HIM). Ekadasi means number eleven (Eka – One, Dasi – Ten). It can be observed even today that people try to fast on the eleventh day during the period of full moon and no moon. In my opinion, Ekadasi Upavasam is not just meant to be performed during those specific days but is a way of living that one needs to inculcate in daily practice. Controlling all eleven senses every day and contemplating HIM will eventually lead to the path of eternal happiness and attain HIS supreme abode.

While I will not go deep into mathematics, it can be observed that when the world is struggling to calculate numbers beyond 0-9, Sanatana Dharma always had a numbering system in their Vedic scriptures for more than 5000+ years. After number 9, they are counted as Dasa (10), Ekadasa (11), Dwadasa (12), Triodasa (13), Sata (100), Sahasra (1000) and many more. Around the 5th Century, the Indian mathematician and astronomer Aryabhatta used a symbol for ZERO. However, Brahmagupta, another mathematician, formalised the utilisation of ZERO in the 7th Century AD.

धूमेनाव्रियते वह्निर्यथादर्शो मलेन च ।
यथोल्बेनावृतो गर्भस्तथा तेनेदमावृतम् ॥

Dhoomenaavriyate Vahniryathaadarsho Malena Cha
Yatholbenaavruto Garbhastatha Tenedamaavrutam

Krishna explains with excellent examples to clear all the confusion. The above verse means, just like smoke covers the fire, dust covers the mirror, and amniotic fluid covers the Baby in the mother's womb, Desires, Lust and

Anger cover the Soul. One can see the Soul only by overcoming such Desires, Lust, and Anger which is possible with the Ekadasi upavasam or Ekadasi Vratam (controlling eleven senses).

It is difficult to stay away from them, so people are never satisfied with what they possess. Their greed to possess more, forces them to commit more sins.

As mentioned earlier, the senses (the ten elements) are superior to human beings. The Mind is superior to the ten Senses. The Soul is Superior to the Mind. To see the Soul and attain Moksha, realise the Soul and gain victory over the senses and Mind.

एवं बुद्धेः परं बुद्ध्वा संस्तभ्यात्मानमात्मना ।

जहि शत्रुं महाबाहो कामरूपं दुरासदम् ॥

Evam Budhdhoha Param Buddhva
Samstabhyaatmaanamaatmmanaa

Jahi shatrum mahaabaaho kaamaroopam duraasadam

Hence, Krishna suggests that Arjuna eliminate the attachment towards the senses and Mind and understand the supremacy of the Atma (Soul).

During this conversation, Krishna established the importance of performing the duties while staying disconnected from the results or desires of the outcome. The responsibilities performed for righteousness without the desire for the outcome and with a sense of offering back to nature (Divine Gods), one will still attain the Moksha. Hence, Arjuna was asked to stand up against the evil (Adharma) and fight the battle.

Krishna is the Maker of Law and Order. He created this universe (which we will learn in the upcoming chapters). When the demonic senses take over the Justice, he commands Arjuna to perform his duty as a Law keeper. Arjuna, being a warrior, must fulfil his actions and restore the Justice.

Law and Order are meant to punish people who commit sins. If the Law orders a death sentence for a criminal, the Law must retain Justice. However, if a normal human being performs criminal activities, it is not considered righteousness (Dharma).

In my opinion, the invaluable gift that God gave to Humankind is the sense of understanding and realisation. Animals or nature don't have that sense of emotions. They perform their duties diligently. Unfortunately, humans are attached to desires, lust, and anger and often misuse their capabilities to commit irreversible sins like Duryodhana did in the Mahabharata.

Chapter 4
Gyana Yoga (Essence of Wisdom)

श्रीभगवानुवाच ।
इमं विवस्वते योगं प्रोक्तवानहमव्ययम् ।
विवस्वान्मनवे प्राह मनुरिक्ष्वाकवेऽब्रवीत् ॥

Imam Vivasvate Yogam Praaktavaanahamavyayam
Vivasvaanmanave Praaha Manurikshvaakavebraveet

Many can challenge who documented the Vedic knowledge thousands of years ago and how it is preserved and spread across the Humankind.

In the following verses, Krisha confirms that HE provided this wisdom to Lord Sun. Then, that was subsequently taught to King Ikshvaka (the forefathers of Lord Sri Ram), and from there, through many Teachers (Gurus), it was passed on to generation after generation.

As the time lapsed, the essence and knowledge of Vedas faded away. Observing the situation, the great sage

Vedavyasa (incarnation of Sri Maha Vishnu) rewrote Asthadasa (18) Puranas and Bhagavat Gita, which is part of the great epic Mahabharata, to help humankind follow.

अर्जुन उवाच ।

अपरं भवतो जन्म परं जन्म विवस्वतः ।

कथमेतद्विजानीयां त्वमादौ प्रोक्तवानिति ॥

Arjuna Uvacha

Aparam Bhavato Janma Param Janma Vivasvataha

Kathametadvijaaneeyam Tvamaadou Proktavaaniti

Surprised, Arjuna asks Krishna, "Since the Sun God has existed for millions of years, how can Krishna bestow this knowledge?"

According to some calculations, at the time of the Mahabharata war, Arjuna was around 70 years old, and Krishna was a few years older than him. Arjuna assumes that since Krishna had only existed for a limited time, then how could he imbibe the Vedas to the Sun God, who existed for millions of years?

श्रीभगवानुवाच ।

बहूनि मे व्यतीतानि जन्मानि तव चार्जुन ।

तान्यहं वेद सर्वाणि न त्वं वेत्थ परन्तप ॥

Sri Bhagavan Uvacha

Bahooni Ma Vyateetaani Janmaani Tava Chaarjuna

Taanyaham Veda Sarvaani Na Tvam Vettha Parantapa

Dear Arjuna, we were born multiple times in the past. However, I have the ability to remember everything, but you do not.

Assume the situation in which we remember our past lives. The emotions and attachments of past life will make the current life miserable. Forgetfulness is one of the best gifts that God has given to Humankind in such a situation. Krishna reaffirms the concept of rebirth and establishes that Krishna has been there forever.

अजोऽपि सन्नव्ययात्मा भूतानामीश्वरोऽपि सन् ।

प्रकृतिं स्वामधिष्ठाय सम्भवाम्यात्ममायया ॥

Ajopi Sannavyayaatmaa Bhootaanaameeswaropi san

Prakrutim Svaamadhisthaaya Sambhavaamyaatmamaayayaa

Krishna continues, 'While my divine form has no birth or death. However, with my eternal powers, I incarnate in every Yuga'.

यदा यदा हि धर्मस्य ग्लानिर्भवति भारत ।

अभ्युत्थानमधर्मस्य तदात्मानं सृजाम्यहम् ॥

Yadaa Yadaa HiDharmasya Glanirbhavati Bhaarata

Abhyuththanam Adharmasya Tadaatmaanam Srujaamyaham

Wherever and whenever, righteousness (Dharma) is threatened and injustice prevail, I will descend to this material world to bring back Justice.

परित्राणाय साधूनां विनाशाय च दुष्कृताम् ।

धर्मसंस्थापनार्थाय सम्भवामि युगे युगे ॥

Pavitraanaya Saadunaam VinaasaayaCha Dushkrutaam

Dharma Samsthaapanaarthaya Sambhavami Yuge Yuge

To protect the saints and destroy demonic people, I take birth again and again across different Yugas.

काङ्क्षन्तः कर्मणां सिद्धिं यजन्त इह देवताः ।

क्षिप्रं हि मानुषे लोके सिद्धिर्भवति कर्मजा ॥

धर्मसंस्थापनाथामय सम्भवामर् युगे युगे

Kaamkshantaha karmaanaamsiddhim yajasta
iha devataaha
Kshipram Hi Manushe Loke Sidharbhavati Karmajaa

People who perform their prayers to the gods and demigods for their worldly desires will gain those results quickly in this life.

Since he is the supreme power, he created the whole universe with his simple idea. Everything belongs to him. Since everything is created by him, HE does not require anything. He has no desires, is not greedy, and is not influenced by materialistic offerings.

People are unable to differentiate between acceptable Do's and Don'ts. Those who differentiate between the two and are free from attachments to the results are considered Saintly human beings.

All HE needs is a devoted mind and living with righteousness. Live by the Law of nature.

चातुर्वर्ण्यं मया सृष्टं गुणकर्मविभागशः ।
तस्य कर्तारमपि मां विद्ध्यकर्तारमव्ययम् ॥

Chaaturvarnyam Mayaa Srustham
Junakarmavibhaagasaha
Tastha Kartaaramapi Maam Viddhyakartaaramavyayam

I created the four races based on human nature and their associated duties. Though I created such bifurcation, consider me, as I am not attached to such activities or duties.

It is often misinterpreted widely that the races are bifurcated to discriminate between the Brahman (Priest), Kshatriya (Kings), Vaishya (Business Men) and Sudra (Daily Labour). Krishna created them to distinguish between various duties performed by those sects. Over the years, people have used such bifurcation for their own benefit and have tried suppressing one another. For Krishna, all human beings are the same.

न मां कर्माणि लिम्पन्ति न मे कर्मफले स्पृहा ।

इति मां योऽभिजानाति कर्मभिर्न स बध्यते ॥

Na Maam Karmaani Limpanthi Na Me Karmaphale Spruhaa

Iti Maam Yobhjaanaati Karmabhrna Sa Bandhate

None of the materialistic duties can control or attach me to the results. Those who understand such a supreme Soul of mine will not be connected to the outcomes of their duties.

ब्रह्मार्पणं ब्रह्म हविर्ब्रह्माग्नौ ब्रह्मणा हुतम् ।

ब्रह्मैव तेन गन्तव्यं ब्रह्मकर्मसमाधिना ॥

Brahmaarpanam Brahma Havirbrahmaagnou
Brahmanaa Hutam
Brahmaiva Tena Gantavyam Brahmakarma
Samaadhinaa

Krishna mentions that sacrificing the results to Brahma (the supreme lord) will help people detach from worldly attachments. Just by sacrificing the results to the lord, it relieves humankind from materialistic bonds.

Money offered to a person in need, the right over the value is relinquished by the giver and should not expect anything in return. However, if the act is motivated by greed or desire for a favour, it indicates the attachment to the outcome. When the recipient fails to meet those expectations, the giver may experience emotional distress such as anger or anxiety, thus becoming trapped in the circle of attachment and suffering.

I believe Sanatana Dharma often taught sacrificing the proceedings of the Yagna to Supreme power by chanting Samvarm Parabhrahmarpanam Astu, Sarvam Sri Parvati Parameswararpanamastu, Sarvam Sri Lakshmi Narayanarpanamastu, or Sarvam Sri Krishnarpanamastu. (I offer the proceedings of the prayers or yagna to the Supreme Power)

Some people perform deep Penance and yagnas, some recite Vedic hymns, some listen to such hymns and control their five senses, some control their desires and lusts generated out of the five senses and try to realise their inner Soul, and some perform intense prayers. Some concentrate at the top of their nose, by closing their eyes, and perform intense meditation to attain the supremacy in meditation and Moksha.

If one performs their duties as prescribed above, one will soon attain heavenly abode.

अज्ञश्चाश्रद्दधानश्च संशयात्मा विनश्यति ।
नायं लोकोऽस्ति न परो न सुखं संशयात्मनः ॥

Agyanamschasradhadhaanascha Samsayaatmaa Vinasyati
Naayam Lokosthi Na Paro Sukham Samsayaatmanaha

Those who suspect the Vedic scriptures and are disinterested in understanding such divine knowledge will never be satisfied or happy, either in this materialistic world or in heaven or hell.

Therefore, try to dispel your illusions, uphold righteousness, and attain the path to divine abode.

Chapter 5

Karma Sanyasa Yoga (Essence of actions with detachment)

अर्जुन उवाच ।

संन्यासं कर्मणां कृष्ण पुनर्योगं च शंससि ।

यच्छ्रेय एतयोरेकं तन्मे ब्रूहि सुनिश्चितम् ॥

Arjuna Uvacha

Sanyaasam Karmanaam Krushna Punaryogam cha Shamsasi

Yachreya Etayorekam Tanme Bruhi Sunischitam

Arjuna enquiries, is it better to be enlightened and live like a saint or perform the duties?

In the last two chapters, Krishana recommended performing duties while stressing the importance of enlightenment or Guyana yoga. Arjuna is looking for a precise answer. Most of the time, when we are in a dilemma between multiple options, we always seek guidance about the right decision. Similarly, Arjuna seeks a recommendation from Krishna to clearly state the best choice for him (our humankind).

श्रीभगवानुवाच ।

संन्यासः कर्मयोगश्च निःश्रेयसकरावुभौ ।

तयोस्तु कर्मसंन्यासात्कर्मयोगो विशिष्यते ॥

Sri Bhagavan Uvacha

Sanyasaha Karmayogascha Nihi Sreyaskaravubhou

Tayostu Karmasanyaasaat Karmayogo vishisthate

Krishna says, 'Both executing duties with sincerity and devotion as well as surrendering the duties completely and living with spirituality like a saint will lead to liberation (Moksha).' However, performing duties with devotion is a better option. As said earlier, those who perform their duties with passion and detachment to the outcome will be freed from the dual facet attachments.

In the materialistic world, actions with strong desires always have dual-facet results. Nature performs its duties without expecting anything in return. For example, trees provide fruits and oxygen without expecting any rewards.

योगयुक्तो विशुद्धात्मा विजितात्मा जितेन्द्रियः ।
सर्वभूतात्मभूतात्मा कुर्वन्नपि न लिप्यते ॥

Yogayukto Vishuddhatmaa Vijitaatma Jitendriyaha
Sarvabhootatma Bhootatmaa Kurvannapi na Lipyate

Those who perform duties with devotion, control their senses, and arc detached from the outcomes, which leads to liberation. Krishna relates those who perform their duties with a sense of devotion, are like the water droplets on the lotus leaf. Just like the water droplets do not stick to the lotus leaf, a true transcendental person is detached from the outcomes. On the other hand, illiterates assume that they are in control of every outcome and are the reason for success or failure. Such people wander in the circle of Life.

The term "illiterate" does not mean uneducated. It refers to those who may be intellects but are attached to materialistic desires and self-esteem. Look at Duryodhana. He is intelligent and well-educated; however, he utilises all his knowledge to take over the wealth and happiness of the Pandavas.

In the competitive world, people often strive to grow faster and accumulate wealth. They may feel redundant if they are not in the race and feel worthless in the workplace or their social circle. Wealth is acceptable when earned in all fairness. However, success achieved through demeaning others is unethical.

He also emphasises that humankind cannot run away from their duties. Ultimate happiness is in recognising the Soul, and detachment from worldly desires will lead to the path of the Supreme Lord. Therefore, Krishna suggests that Arjuna perform his Duty.

विद्याविनयसम्पन्ने ब्राह्मणे गवि हस्तिनि ।
शुनि चैव श्वपाके च पण्डिताः समदर्शिनः ॥

Vidyaa Vinaya Sampanne Brahmane Gavi Hastini
Shuni Chiva Swapaakecha Panditaah Samadarsinaha

बाह्यस्पर्शेष्वसक्तात्मा विन्दत्यात्मनि यत्सुखम् ।
स ब्रह्मयोगयुक्तात्मा सुखमक्षयमश्नुते ॥

Baahya Sparshevasaktaatmaa Vindathaatmani Yastukham
Sa Brahmayoga Yuktaatmaa Sukhamakshayamasnute

Educated and enlightened people will treat all humankind equally. *This is the most powerful verse in this chapter.*

It is convenient to hate our enemies and love the near and dear. It is complicated to treat everyone equally, irrespective of near and dear, caste and creed, race and ethnicity, rich or poor, or literate or illiterate.

Krishna recommends unbiased ways of living and equal rights for everyone and does not tolerate discrimination. The five elements of the Universe, Earth, Water, Air, Fire, or Wind, never discriminate.

In my view, if I must relate to the business world, when leaders differentiate between core team members and outsiders, it can lead to disruption and pose a significant risk of losing key talent. If the teacher (Guru) discriminates between the students, they may lose interest in education or develop hatred among fellow students causing distress. Treating everyone equally, nurturing and supporting their growth is essential for building a future generations and successful leader. Harmony is crucial in day-to-day Life.

Trying to correlate different incarnations of Lord Vishnu, He was incarnated as an Animal, such as a Fish (Mastya), Tortoise (Kurma), Boar (Varaha), half-man half-Lion (Narasimha) and then born as a Brahmin (Vamana and Parasurama), Kshatriya (Rama – The King), or Yadava (Krishna). He took so many forms in different classes. When the supreme personality (Vishnu) himself does not discriminate, who are we?

According to Bhagavata Puranam, the size of the Earth is the size of a mustard seed at the top of the center hood of the countless (1000) hooded snake (Aadisheh) bed on which Sri Mahavishnu (Krishna) sleeps in his meditating state (Yoganidra).

Imagine how insignificant size of the Earth and the invisible size of the human being in this galaxy. However, human beings are full of ego, desires, lust, and anger claiming the credit for such petty accomplishments in the short span of Life and living with pride – ME, MYSELF, and MY FAMILY.

According to the Puranas, He covers the whole Universe. Is it possible to travel so far and visualise and document what they have seen physically? In the upcoming chapters, Krishna clarifies that one can travel beyond this Universe with the help of deep meditation. Rishis, who followed the path of the Vedic scriptures (guide), could visualise such marvels and achievements through meditation. What else can be desired beyond such eternal bliss?

Righteousness is supreme, so Krishna recommends that Arjuna rise above material bliss, fight the battle, and attain eternal happiness.

Chapter 6

Dhyana Yogam (Essence of Meditation)

श्रीभगवानुवाच ।

अनाश्रितः कर्मफलं कार्यं कर्म करोति यः ।

स संन्यासी च योगी च न निरग्निर्न चाक्रियः ॥

Sri Bhagavan Uvacha

Anaasritaha Karmaphalam Karyam Karma Karoti Yaha

Sa Sanyasee Cha Yogee Cha Na Niragnir Na Chaakriyaha

Krishna says, 'Those who perform their duties without attachment are the true Saints. Detaching oneself from responsibilities such as Yagna or duties is not considered a Sage (Saint).

At every stage, Krishna reinstated the importance of performing duties. Arjuna is receiving the timeless teachings just before beginning of the greatest battle. Bhagavad Gita is not meant to be read in the last stages of Life or after retirement. It is a comprehensive guide that recommends the best ways of living for humankind. It provides clear direction and suggestions for day-to-day Life and builds a strong and positive personality.

It is essential to forgo attachment to the five senses, eliminate desire, perform duties with devotion, and become a Spiritual person.

For millions of years, Sanatana Dharma has advocated realising eternal bliss and living for the ultimate happiness to reach the Supreme Abode (where there are no dual facet attachments). It is all about pleasant and happy souls wandering around the supreme Power with devotion.

उद्धरेदात्मनात्मानं नात्मानमवसादयेत् ।

आत्मैव ह्यात्मनो बन्धुरात्मैव रिपुरात्मनः ॥

Uddharedaatmanaatmaanam Natmaanamavasaadayet

Aatmaevahyaatmano Bandhuratmeyvaripuraatmanaha

बन्धुरात्मात्मनस्तस्य येनात्मैवात्मना जितः ।

अनात्मनस्तु शत्रुत्वे वर्तेतात्मैव शत्रुवत् ॥

Bandhuratmaatmanastasya Yenatmeyvaatmanaa Jitaha

Anaatmanastu Shtruve Vrtetaathmeva Satruvat

Humankind must try to progress towards detaching from their desires while executing their duties. As they practice detachment, they will not be influenced by the outcome. Once people reach transcendental state of mind, they will have complete control over their minds.

Those who are attached to the results behave like their own enemy. The never-ending search for fulfilling more desires can lead to committing sins. Hence, Krishna says, 'Your Mind Is Your Biggest Enemy.' If one can control their mind and Soul will become pure. Therefore, rise beyond these desires and purify one's Soul.

सुहृन्मित्रार्युदासीनमध्यस्थद्वेष्यबन्धुषु ।
साधुष्वपि च पापेषु समबुद्धिर्विशिष्यते ॥

Suhrunmitraaryudaaseenamadhyasthadveshyabandhushu
Saadhushvapi Cha Paapeshu Samabudhirvishyate

Those who treat well-wishers, friends, enemies, haters, good and bad, with equality are advanced in their path towards purifying their souls. External factors will not influence their mind and Soul.

In the last five chapters, Krishna suggested that realising the Soul is the ultimate happiness while the physical body is temporary and short-lived. Realising the Soul is difficult until someone discharges himself from materialistic desires and detachment from the five senses. As people leave such desires behind, Krishna explains the purpose of humankind's existence and how one must conduct oneself to attain supreme spirituality.

योगी युञ्जीत सततमात्मानं रहसि स्थितः ।
एकाकी यतचित्तात्मा निराशीरपरिग्रहः ॥

Yogee Yungneeta Satatamaatmaanam Rahasi Sthitaha
Ekaaki Yatachittaatma Niraaseeraparigrahaha

Such a spiritual individual should concentrate on the supreme Power (God) while living in a lonely place with a pleasant mind.

The verse below states how one should try to perform meditation, which will lead the person to the heavens.

शुचौ देशे प्रतिष्ठाप्य स्थिरमासनमात्मनः ।
नात्युच्छ्रितं नातिनीचं चैलाजिनकुशोत्तरम् ॥

Shuchou Desho Pratishaapya Sthiramaasanamaatmanaha
Natyuchchritam Naatineecham Chilaajinakusottaram

तत्रैकाग्रं मनः कृत्वा यतचित्तेन्द्रियक्रियः ।
उपविश्यासने युञ्ज्याद्योगमात्मविशुद्धये ॥

Tatrekaagram manaha krutvaa Yatachittendriyakriyaha
Upavishyaasane Yungyaad Yogamaatma Vishudhraye

Krishna describes the place of meditation to help achieve spiritual state. Identify a pleasant, clean, and isolated place. Place the sacred grass (Darbha) on top of it, then the deer skin on top of it, and finally, a soft cloth to make a comfortable seat. Rest on top of that seat in a folded leg (Padmasana), controlling all the senses and mind, and concentrate on a single point at the top of the nose to start meditation.

समं कायशिरोग्रीवं धारयन्नचलं स्थिरः ।
सम्प्रेक्ष्य नासिकाग्रं स्वं दिशश्चानवलोकयन् ॥

Samam Kaayasirogreevam Dharayannchalam Sthiraha
Sampresha Naasikaagram Swam Dishchaanavalokayan

प्रशान्तात्मा विगतभीर्ब्रह्मचारिव्रते स्थितः ।
मनः संयम्य मच्चित्तो युक्त आसीत मत्परः ॥

Prashaantaatmaa vigatabheebrahmachaareevrate sthitaha
Manah samyamya macchitto Yukta Aaseet Matparaha

Keeping the back, neck and head in a straight line, detaching from the pleasures of sex and worldly desires, one should concentrate on the top of the nose. Then, try slowly transferring the concentration to the inner self to feel the divine Power.

नात्यश्नतस्तु योगोऽस्ति न चैकान्तमनश्नतः ।
न चातिस्वप्नशीलस्य जाग्रतो नैव चार्जुन ॥

Naatyasnatasthu Yogoosthi na Chaikaantamanasnataha
Na Chaatiswapnaseelassya Jaagrato Naivachaarjuna

Krishna is providing insights into the 'good and healthy' habits of those willing to take the path of meditation.

Those who eat too much or too little, those who sleep for a long duration, or those who do not sleep enough will not be able succeed in the transcendental journey.

Controlling overeating and sleeping will keep the mind pleasant. With such a pleasant mind, it is easy to concentrate on meditation. Meditating religiously with a steady mindset and consistency makes it easy to attain spirituality and Moksha.

Krishna is suggesting how to lead Life. Practicing good habits like controlling food intake and healthy sleep will help lead a healthy life. Nowadays, every dietitian charge massive fees and guides people about a balanced diet, sleep, exercise and rest. Many years ago, through the Bhagavad Gita, Krishna suggested balanced sleeping and eating. Every verse of the Gita is eternal, irrespective of the evolution of the human race. We may travel to the Moon, Mars, or even farther in the Galaxy; it is impossible to travel to the end of the Universe and visualise the Supreme Power. Such visualisation can only happen with divine meditation and spiritual journey, which the Sages have accomplished it millions of years ago.

It is no brainer to say that one must be consistent while performing their duties diligently to become successful. It will be difficult for an inconsistent performer to be successful, whether in education, a career in the corporate world or in sports who is inconsistent. People recognise and appreciate those who are consistent.

Current chapter of meditation (Dhyana Yoga) also suggests the same.

यतो यतो निश्चरति मनश्चञ्चलमस्थिरम् ।
ततस्ततो नियम्यैतदात्मन्येव वशं नयेत् ॥

Yato Yato Nishcharati Manashchanchalamsthitam
Tatastato Niyamyitadaatmanyeva Vasam Nayet

It is obvious that by nature, the mind wanders. One should bring back the thoughts, continue to control the mind, and concentrate on the inner Soul.

सर्वभूतस्थमात्मानं सर्वभूतानि चात्मनि ।
ईक्षते योगयुक्तात्मा सर्वत्र समदर्शनः ॥

Sarvabhootasthamaatmanam Sarvabhootaanichaatmaani
Eekshite Yogayuktaatmaa Srvatra Samadarshanaha

The genuine spiritual person will find ME (Krishna - the God) everywhere.

Now, slowly, Krishna establishes himself as the Supreme Power (the God) who controls this, Universe.

It is no brainer to state that some supreme natural power controls this Universe and ensures the planets revolve in their restricted area and do not deviate from their orbit. The Sages named supernatural powers Vishnu, Brahma, Siva, Lakshmi, Saraswati, Durga, Ganesh, Skanda and many more. The Gita is delivered by Krishan, the incarnation of Vishnu, to provide the everlasting guide to humankind.

I often observed people questioning Sanatana Dharma having millions of gods. In my perspective when a man-made organisation requires 100s of people to run its business to be successful; for the Universe to operate in its orbit and perform its duties, without colliding with each other, it requires supernatural powers to control them. We may call them magnetic powers, cosmic energies or any other scientific term.

Imagine the Sun God deviates from his orbit (prescribed position) and travels closer or farther to Earth. Imagine

Earth stops rotating. The Sanatana Dharma provided specific names to those supernatural powers that control the Universe.

The companies may or may not be successful or cease to exist someday, but for the Universe, there is no scope for failure. Otherwise, it will be a devastation.

Similarly, these supernatural powers influence people's minds and lives. The oceans have high impacts and tides on a Full Moon or No Moon Day. These influences affect people's minds on those specific days and can be visibly observed in few people.

This confirms that supernatural powers and planets directly impact human beings. Sanatana Dharma provided these details to perfection in the Vedas (Sacred Scriptures). Such supernatural powers are given specific names and build stories around to implant the knowledge from the childhood days in India.

As stated in the previous chapters, the sounds emerge while chanting the Vedas act as the communication channel to respective supernatural (Cosmic) power which influences the characteristics and behaviour of human beings.

After listening to Krishna with such devotion, Arjuna now asks –

अर्जुन उवाच।

योऽयं योगस्त्वया प्रोक्तः साम्येन मधुसूदन।

एतस्याहं न पश्यामि चञ्चलत्वात्स्थितिं स्थिराम्॥

Arjuna Uvacha

Yoyam Yogastvayaa Proktaha Saamyena Madhusoodana

Etasyaaham Na Pasyami Chamchalatwaat Sthitam Sthiraam

चञ्चलं हि मनः कृष्ण प्रमाथि बलवद् दृढम्।

तस्याहं निग्रहं मन्ये वायोरिव सुदुष्करम्॥

Chanchalam hi Manah Krishna Pramaathi Balavadrhurdham

Sasyaaham Nigraham Manye Vaayoriva Sudushkaram

"The Mind is powerful, flickering, and turbulent. Restricting such a mind can be referred to as controlling the Air with our hands, which is impossible."

Earlier, Arjuna was requesting Krishna to tell him a definitive course of action whether to fight the battle or not. However, he is slowly moving towards discovering his inner self to attain Moksha. It can be observed that his mindset is changing from the core result of the war.

श्रीभगवानुवाच ।

असंशयं महाबाहो मनो दुर्निग्रहं चलम् ।

अभ्यासेन तु कौन्तेय वैराग्येण च गृह्यते ॥

Sri Bhagavan Uvacha

Asamsayam Mahaabaaho ManoDurnigraham Chalam

AbhaasenaTu Kounteya Vairaagyena Cha Gruhyate

Krishna says, "Of course, Arjuna, the mind is powerful, turbulent, and difficult to control. However, it can still be controlled with dedication, consistent practice, and detachment."

असंयतात्मना योगो दुष्प्राप इति मे मतिः ।

वश्यात्मना तु यतता शक्योऽवाप्तुमुपायतः ॥

Asamyataatmanaa Yogo Dushpraapa Iti Me Matihi

Vasyaatmanaa Tu Yatataa Sakyovaaptumupaayataha

It is challenging for those who cannot control their minds to realise their souls. But it is quite possible for those individuals who win over their desires and mind.

As stated in the previous chapter, if one can control the eleven senses, including the mind and detach from worldly desires, it becomes easy for someone to attain Moksha.

अर्जुन उवाच ।

अयतिः श्रद्धयोपेतो योगाच्चलितमानसः ।

अप्राप्य योगसंसिद्धिं कां गतिं कृष्ण गच्छति ॥

Arjuna Uvacha

Ayatihi Sradhdhayopeto Yojaachchalitamaanasaha

Apraapya Yogasamsidhim KaamKatim Krishna Gachchati

कच्चिन्नोभयविभ्रष्टश्छिन्नाभ्रमिव नश्यति ।

अप्रतिष्ठो महाबाहो विमूढो ब्रह्मणः पथि ॥

Kachchinnobhayavibhrashtuschinnaabhamiva Nasyati

Apratishto Mahaabaho Vimoodho Brahmanaha Pathihi

It may not be possible for every individual to realise their Soul and consistently perform the Penance forever. People might want to go through the path of devotion with the help of meditation. However, they may become inconsistent and need to fulfil worldly desires due to many influencing factors.

It is a common situation for the majority of the people. Arjuna is asking what happens to such people like us. Neither are they entirely on the journey of self-realisation (Soul Realisation) nor are they attached to their desires. He believes they are left nowhere.

श्रीभगवानुवाच ।

पार्थ नैवेह नामुत्र विनाशस्तस्य विद्यते ।

न हि कल्याणकृत्कश्चिद् दुर्गतिं तात गच्छति ॥

Sri Bhagavan Uvacha

Paartha Naiveha Naamutra Vinaasastasya Vidyate

Na Hi Kalyaanakrutkaschida Durgatim Taata Gachchati

Krishna relieves Arjuna (us) by stating, 'Those who perform good deeds and work towards self-realisation with devotion, their efforts will never go vein'. There is no destruction for them in this world or the spiritual world.

प्राप्य पुण्यकृतां लोकानुषित्वा शाश्वतीः समाः ।

शुचीनां श्रीमतां गेहे योगभ्रष्टोऽभिजायते ॥

Praapya Punyakrutaam Lokaanushitvaa
saashvatihi samaaha
Sucheenaam sreemataam Gehe Yogabhrashtobhijaayate

Such unsuccessful Yogi (spiritual Soul), after spending many years of enjoyment in the heavens, will be reborn in this materialistic world in the families of affluent or well-behaved/educated.

पूर्वाभ्यासेन तेनैव ह्रियते ह्यवशोऽपि सः ।
जिज्ञासुरपि योगस्य शब्दब्रह्मातिवर्तते ॥

Poorvaabhaasena tenaiva Hriyate Hyavashopi saha
Jigynaasurapi Yogasya Sabdabrahmaativartate

Because of the good deeds from the previous Life and divine consciousness of the Soul, the newly reborn will naturally get attracted to those good deeds and devotion towards the supreme Power *(Remember, the Soul travels from one body to the other).* After living such numerable lives, one will entirely devote himself, become an absolute saint (doesn't have to perform any duty), and attain the supreme abode forever. Time and again, Sanatana Dharma establishes firm trust in rebirth.

तपस्विभ्योऽधिको योगी ज्ञानिभ्योऽपि मतोऽधिकः ।
कर्मिभ्यश्चाधिको योगी तस्माद्योगी भवार्जुन ॥

Tapasvibhyodhiko Yogee Gyanibhyopi Matodhikaha
Karmibhyaschaadhiko Yogee Tasmaadyogee
Bhavaarjuna

The Yogi is superior to the divine meditator, an enlightened and Duty-minded.

Once recognising such a Supreme Power (Krishna) everywhere, there is nothing else to hate or love. Such an individual is considered as transcendental. Such Yogi finds the supreme person within the self and will see everyone as Krishna. Such a person will not curse himself by cursing others.

Those who become Yogis and always think about ME (Krishna) are the most incredible human beings. Such people are scarce and difficult to find. They are near and dear to Krishna, so Krishna suggests Arjuna become a Yogi.

Chapter 7
Bhakti Yoga (Essence of Devotion)

श्रीभगवानुवाच ।

मय्यासक्तमनाः पार्थ योगं युञ्जन्मदाश्रयः ।

असंशयं समग्रं मां यथा ज्ञास्यसि तच्छृणु ॥

Sri Bhagavan Uvacha

Mayyaasaktamanaah Partha Yogam Yunjanmadaasrayaha

Sasamsayaha Samagram Maam Yathaa Gynasyasi Tachrunu

There is nothing else to explore after understanding the completeness of the knowledge (Gyanam) and Wisdom (Vigyanam) about ME. Once people know ME, nothing else is left to be known.

मनुष्याणां सहस्रेषु कश्चिद्यतति सिद्धये ।

यततामपि सिद्धानां कश्चिन्मां वेत्ति तत्त्वतः ॥

Manushyanaam Sahasreshu Kashchidhytati Siddhaye

Yatataamapi Sidhdhaanaam Kashchinmaam Vetti Tatvataha

Recognising and understanding such knowledge entirely is a difficult task. Among thousands (innumerable) of people, only a handful of them will endeavour to understand the supreme knowledge. Out of them, only one or two will realise that 'I am the ultimate Truth'.

Earth, Water, Fire, Air, Sky, Mind, Intelligence, and Self-Esteem (ego) are my eight materialistic forms. Humankind cannot exist without these eight key elements, and I confirm that I am the source of everything. These eight elements have a limited lifespan by nature, however, there is a different power that exists beyond these.

एतद्योनीनि भूतानि सर्वाणीत्युपधारय ।

अहं कृत्स्नस्य जगतः प्रभवः प्रलयस्तथा ॥

Etat Yoneeni Bhootani Sarvaanit Upadhaaraya

Aham Krurtsnasya Jagataha Prabhavaha Pralayastatha

I am the Creator and the destroyer of both Materialistic and Spiritual worlds. There is nothing superior to ME. I exist in every materialistic and spiritual being similar how the thread in the garland of beads exists in every bead.

Imagine each living being as a bead in a garland, with Krishna as the thread that connects them all. As long as our minds and souls remain connected to him, humanity is well-protected. However, if we sever this connection, we will scatter like beads from a broken garland, lacking order and discipline.

Krishna explains his existence and abilities and supremacy among different materialistic forms that humankind experience in their day-to-day life. I tried to simplify and tried to provide the summary in a tabular form for an easy understanding.

Materialistic Form	**The Power (Krishna)**
In the Water	I am the Taste
In the Sun and Moon	I am the Light
In the Vedas	I am the Sound of Aum (The very first word of Vedas)
In the Sky	I am the sound
In the Human being	I am the Ability
In the Earth	I am the smell
In the Fire	I am the Warmth or heat

In the Living Beings	I am the Life
In the Saints (Yogis)	I am the Penance
In all the living beings	I am the seed
In the Intellects	I am the Intelligence
The Powerful people	I am the Power
In the Strong People	I am the strength except for the unlawful desires
In the Satva (Good), Rajo (Passion and Lust) and Tamo (Anger or Ignorance) Gunas	I am the source of all such characteristics in humans

As referred to above, Krishna exists everywhere.

Everything emerged out of ME; however, neither these elements can ever control ME, nor I am attached to them.

It isn't easy to overcome from Satvarajastamo gunas. However, those who are entirely devoted to ME can easily conquer them.

The ignorant who are with diabolical mindset, will never be able to realise this form of mine and will never be able to reach ME (Attain ultimate happiness – Moksha).

All the devotees are kind people without any doubt in some form or another. There is no difference between those people and myself, who understand my absolute form. Such people evolve themselves as transcendental through different births and reach my supreme abode in the end. Such people are scarce.

People may question if Krishna is everything, why people pray to different deities, and what happens to those who are devoted to them.

People pray to different deities as per their will and wish. I will bestow their desires through such deities. However, in the end, they all will reach me.

Krishna also establishes and eliminates the illusion of such people who believe the Supreme Power has no form and consider Krishna or any of his incarnation on this materialistic world as a normal human being. Such people will never be able to understand HIS Divine form or Powers.

वेदाहं समतीतानि वर्तमानानि चार्जुन ।
भविष्याणि च भूतानि मां तु वेद न कश्चन ॥

Vedhaaham Samateetaani Vartamaanaani Charjuna
Bhavishaani Bhootaani Maam Tu Veda Na Kaschin

I know everything that happened in the past, is happening in the present and will happen in the future. Similarly, I observe every human being, but they cannot recognise my Divine form. There is nothing that I do not know. Irrespective of the past, present and future, I remember everything.

People can challenge how Krishna can know every person. As he pointed out earlier in this chapter, he lives in every living being as a thread in a garland of beads. He is the lifeline of every human being hence, he is aware of everything.

When people realise that Krishna exists everywhere, no one will dare to commit misconduct, hate, or curse others (except the ignorant people who abide by unlawful desires).

साधिभूताधिदैवं मां साधियज्ञं च ये विदुः ।
प्रयाणकालेऽपि च मां ते विदुर्युक्तचेतसः ॥

Saathibhutaadhidyivam maam saadhiyagnyam cha ye viduhu
Prayaanakaalepi cha maam te viduryuktachetasaha

Those who recognise that I am the Creator, administrator and destructor of this material and the celestial world and are devoted towards me will reach me at the end of their lives.

Chapter 8

Bhagavad Praapti (Journey towards Supreme)

अर्जुन उवाच ।

किं तद् ब्रह्म किमध्यात्मं किं कर्म पुरुषोत्तम ।

अधिभूतं च किं प्रोक्तमधिदैवं किमुच्यते ॥

Arjuna Uvacha

Kim Tad Brahma Kim Adyatmam Kim Karma Purushettam

Adhibhootam cha Kim Proktam Adidaivam Kimuchchate

अधियज्ञः कथं कोऽत्र देहेऽस्मिन्मधुसूदन ।

प्रयाणकाले च कथं ज्ञेयोऽसि नियतात्मभिः ॥

Adhiyagyaha Katham Kotra Dehesmin Madhusudhana

Rayaanakaale Cha Katham Gneyosi Niyataatmabhihi

What is the definition of Adibhoota Adidaiva and Adhiyagyna? How will the Soul reach the ultimate abode after leaving the physical body (The last travel)? Who resides in these souls?

Observe the order of conversation from the beginning. At the beginning, Arjuna was worried about his family and friends. Unclear about his responsibility, he considered possible reasons to avoid the battle. Then, he tried to understand his Duty. Later, he understood the difference between Duty and how to perform his duties with a detachment from worldly desires. With detachment from worldly desires, the mind feels pleasant and starts a journey towards eternal happiness. Such a pleasant mind tried to explore the Supreme Power – Krishna. After learning about Krishna, Arjuna is trying to find the path to reach him. Hence, there are questions about differentiating between the material world, Demigods, and God. How the Supreme God lives in every living creature.

It is not easy to get away from worldly desires and directly associate with the Supreme Power, according to me. It is a journey. One should practice this journey consistently and religiously, dedicating oneself to discovering the Supreme Lord.

Adibhoota is the materialistic world, and Adidaiva is the demigods like the Sun, Moon, Saturn, Mars, etc.

Adhiyagna is none other than Krishna himself. He is the smallest of the small and the largest of the large. I reside in every creature as the Paramatma (Supreme Soul), and the entire Universe is within him. There is nothing that I cannot observe.

Like the rays emerging out from The Sun's or the Moon's leave nothing untouched, there is nothing that Supreme God is unaware of.

Those who consistently think about me, perform their duties devoted to me, and remember me during their last breath will certainly reach my Supreme Abode.

Arjuna, perform your Duty without any desires, devote yourself to me and reach my Supreme Abode instead of wandering around in this material world.

Those who can control all their senses, meditate as prescribed, think about me, chant the Aum while leaving this materialistic world will undoubtedly attain the Supreme Abode.

People may assume that one can perform all the misdeeds and that just chanting Aum or thinking about the Supreme Power will lead them to the Supreme Abode.

For such people, a record is maintained to monitor the good and bad deeds performed by living beings. Those who perform good deeds will certainly attain Supreme Abode. However, once their merits are exhausted, they will return to this material world.

Krishna briefly touches on the concept of the time and age of the planets in the Bhagavad Gita. Srimad Bhagavatam provides a comprehensive explanation about the same.

There are fourteen planets, with Earth at the centre. All these planets are materialistic and are perishable. The Naraka (hell) is at the bottom of all the lokas. There is another place beyond all these, the Supreme Abode, where Lord Vishnu (Krishna—Krishna already established himself as the Supreme Lord—Sri MahaVishnu in the previous chapter) lives.

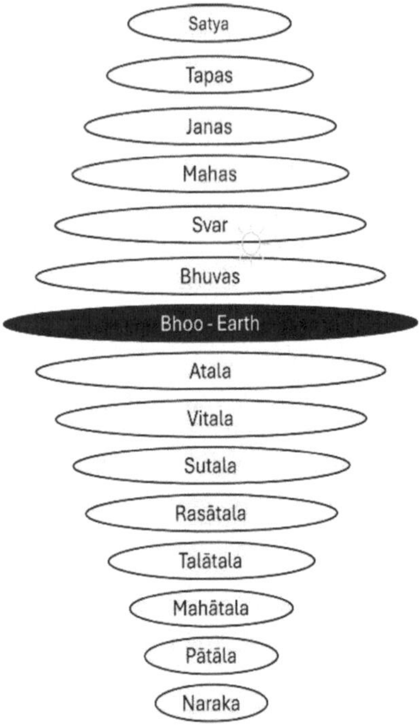

The full calendar year is divided into two halves. One is called Uttarayana (Northern), and the other is Dakshanayana (Southern).

The months - Magha, Phalguna, Chaitra, Vaisakha, Jyestha, Ashadha, Sravana Masas (months) are considered as part of Uttarayana and The Months -

Sravana, Bhadrapada, Aswiyuja, Karthika, Margaseersha and Pushya Masas (months) are considered part of Dakshanayana.

These months are again divided into 15 days of No Moon to Full Moon and 15 days of Full Moon to No Moon, making it 30 days a month.

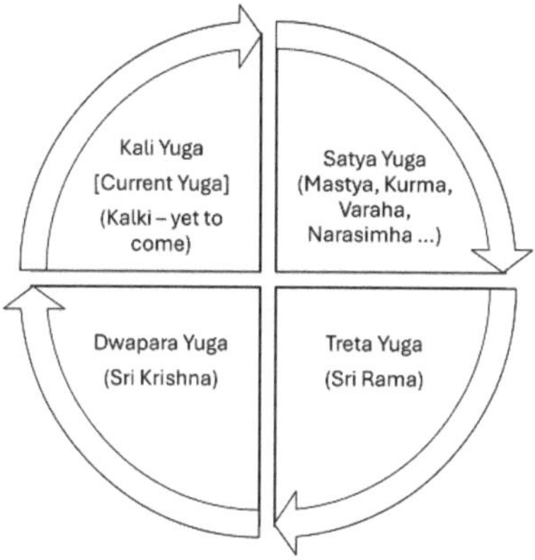

The day and night do not end exactly at the same time every day as they are calculated based on the Sunrise to Sunset, which changes every day.

A high-level calculation of one Kalpa is one day of Brahma (the Creator).

There are fourteen Manvantaras. We are in the 1st Quarter of 7th Manvantara [Vaivasvata– The name of the Manu]. Each Manvantara is divided into four Yugas (quarters). Satya, Treta, Dwapara and Kali Yugas.

Yuga	Years	
Krita (Satya)	17,28,000	
Treta	12,96,000	
Dwapara	864,000	
Kali	432,000	
One Yuga	4,320,000	
71 Yugas	306,720,000	Manvantara
14 Manvantaras	4,294,080,000	Day time of Brahma
15 Manvantaras	25,920,000	Night (Juncture) each night is 17,28,000 years
1 Kalpa	4,320,000,000	

We are in the 7th Manvantara (of 14). Kali Yuga started around 5109 years ago.

Those who leave this material world during the Uttarayana, the Full Moon period of the month, or any other auspicious time as documented in the Vedas will reach the Supreme Abode and never return. Others will return to the earth after completing their stipulated time based on their accomplishments in the past Life.

Learning and studying Vedic sciences, performing sacrifices with intense Penance and meditation, and performing their duties with selflessness and devotion will undoubtedly lead them to the Supreme Abode.

Chapter 9

Rajavidya Rajaguhya Yogam (Knowledge of Hidden Truth)

श्रीभगवानुवाच

राजविद्या राजगुह्यं पवित्रमिदमुत्तमम् ।

प्रत्यक्षावगमं धर्म्यं सुसुखं कर्तुमव्ययम् ॥

Sri Bhagavan Uvacha

Raja vidya Rajaguhyam Pavitram Idam Uttamam

Prathyakshaavagam Dharmyam Susukham Kartumavyayam

Knowledge about the Supreme Lord is the ultimate Wisdom and the secrets of all the secrets.

न च मत्स्थानि भूतानि पश्य मे योगमैश्वरम् ।

भूतभृन्न च भूतस्थो ममात्मा भूतभावनः ॥

Na Cha Matsthani Bhootani Pashya Me Yogamoshvaravam

Bhootabhrunna cha Bhootastho Mamaatma Bhootabhavanaha

Krishna reiterates that he is the Creator of the Universe. I create, administer, and destroy everything that can be seen. I am everywhere and influence the Universe, however, I will not be influenced by them.

We can correlate this message with the rays of the Sun. The properties of the Sun will be in each ray. They will provide sunshine to the universe. The Sun's rays on Earth have many benefits, but he does not need sunshine. He bestows his blessings on humankind without expecting anything in return. All he expects the living beings to live with Dharma.

सर्वभूतानि कौन्तेय प्रकृतिं यान्ति मामिकाम् ।

कल्पक्षये पुनस्तानि कल्पादौ विसृजाम्यहम् ॥

Sarva Bhootani Kaunteya Prakrutim Yaanti Maamikam

Kalpakshayo Punastaani Kalpaadau Visrujaamyaham.

Kalpa consists of 100 years of Lord Brahma. At the end of Kalpa (100 years of Brahma), when it is Time for Brahma to sleep, maha pralaya occurs (master destruction) when the entire Universe submerges into the oceans of galaxies. Then, I will recreate the whole Universe again – The beginning of the new Kalpa.

If we closely observe, this also speaks about the time dilation above this earth. We know the time spent on Moon or Mars by a human being is different from that of the person on earth. Similarly Imagine the supreme powers living beyond this universe. A blink of their eye might be thousands of years on earth. The time dilation was also mentioned in these puranas thousands of years ago.

Supreme God (Krishna) diligently performs his Duty of creation, administration, and destruction; however, he is not emotionally attached to anything that's happening in the Galaxy.

मयाध्यक्षेण प्रकृतिः सूयते सचराचरम् ।
हेतुनानेन कौन्तेय जगद्विपरिवर्तते ॥

Mayaadhyakshena Prakrutihi Suyate Sacharacharam
Hetunaanena Kaunteya Jagadwiparivartate

The entire universe is under my survilance, and its me who creates and destroys it from time to time.

मोघाशा मोघकर्माणो मोघज्ञाना विचेतसः ।

राक्षसीमासुरीं चैव प्रकृतिं मोहिनीं श्रिताः ॥

Moghaasaa Moghakarmano Moghagyaana Vichetasaha
Raakshaseem Aasureem Chaiva Prakrutim Mohineem Shritaha

As I take birth on this planet, Demons, Seculars and Atheists consider me as any other normal humanbeing. Such ignorants are struck in the vicious circle of Life. Their knowledge and contributions goes in vain.

Krishna cites his existence in various forms (purest of the pure).

I am the Kartu – The Doer
I am the Yagna – The sacred penance
I am the Medicine – that fights against illness
I am the Cow Ghee (poured in Yagna)
I am the Fire
I am the Food sacrificed in the Yagna
I am the Father, Mother, Supporter and the Grandfather of this unlimited universe
I am the knowledge
I am the cleanser – purifies soul
I am the sound Aum (The very first verse of the

Vedas)
I am the Rig Yajur Sama and Adharvana Vedas (The four Vedas)
I am the final destination
I am the one who owns all the burden
I am the King
I am the Witness – Since he is everywhere, there is nothing that can be hidden from him. Since he knows everything, he is referred to as the Witness.
I am the Home, or I am the residence
I am a friend
I am the Creator
I am the destructor
I am the seed for everything – The seed that has no end
I am the residing point for everything
I am the reason for the Fire/Heat
I control the rain
I am the nectar
I am the Life, and I am the death
I am the Truth, and I am the non-existence

Those who chant Vedas and delve themselves into spiritual conversations thinking all the time about me, will reach to the heavens. All such acts are recorded to their merit. They will stay in the heaves for a stipulated time and return to the Earth.

अनन्याश्चिन्तयन्तो मां ये जनाः पर्युपासते ।

तेषां नित्याभियुक्तानां योगक्षेमं वहाम्यहम् ॥

Ananyaashintayantho Maam Ye Janaaha Paryupasate

Yeshaam Nityaabhiyuktaanaam Yogakshemam Vahaamyaham

I will protect and fulfil the wishes of my devotees and always keep thinking about them.

पत्रं पुष्पं फलं तोयं यो मे भक्त्या प्रयच्छति ।

तदहं भक्त्युपहृतमश्नामि प्रयतात्मनः ॥

Patram Pushpam Phalam Toyam Yo Me Bhaktyaa Prayachchati

Tadaham Bhatyupahrutamasnami Prayataatmanaha

I accept anything that is offered to me with devotion, whether it is a small Leaf, flower, Fruit or just water.

The whole universe belongs to him. There is nothing that can please him through high value or rich offerings. He accepts even if someone provides a small flower with devotion and love.

All he suggests is to perform the tasks, sacrifice in the Yagna, the Penance, or the meditation with complete dedication, and leave the rest to him. By doing so, one will be freed from the attachments of the results and, in the end, attain Supreme Abode. He doesn't have any partiality towards anyone.

Since I created this Universe, there is nothing that I need to possess, hate or love. My goal is for humankind to live with Dharma. Those who live otherwise need to evolve themselves and take the path towards Dharma to reach me in the end. Those who are devoted to me are my friends, and I am their friend.

Chapter 10

Bhagavad Vibhuti (Magnificence of the Absolute)

श्रीभगवानुवाच ।

भूय एव महाबाहो शृणु मे परमं वचः ।

यत्तेऽहं प्रीयमाणाय वक्ष्यामि हितकाम्यया ॥

Bhooya Yeva Mahabaho Srunume Paramam Vachaha

Yatteham Preeyamaanaaya Vakshyami Hitakaamyayaa

From me arise the qualities of knowledge, wisdom, clarity, forgiveness, truthfulness, mastery over the senses and mind, the experiences of joy and sorrow, the cycles of birth and death, fear and fearlessness, equality, contentment, penance, generosity, nonviolence, and the traits of pride and prejudice. All these characteristics of humanity have evolved from me.

After a detailed explanation of his presence everywhere in the Universe and his supremacy across different powers, Krishna is now explaining how he created and established the Universe.

At the beginning of the universe, the Manu, Sanakasanandasand, and the Seven Maharshis were born out of ME. Further, they expanded all living beings across different planets (as said before, we have 14 planets).

Accordingly, to Sanatana Dharma, the entire world (not just India) is referred to as Vasudaika Kutumbam (the family of Lord Vishnu). There are no geographical borders.

अर्जुन उवाच ।

परं ब्रह्म परं धाम पवित्रं परमं भवान् ।

पुरुषं शाश्वतं दिव्यमादिदेवमजं विभुम् ॥

Arjuna Uvacha

Param Brahma Param Dhaama Pavitram ParamamBhavaan

Purusham Saaswatam Vivyamaadidevamajam Vibhum

आहुस्त्वामृषयः सर्वे देवर्षिर्नारदस्तथा ।

असितो देवलो व्यासः स्वयं चैव ब्रवीषि मे ॥

Aahustwaamruyahaha Sarve Devarshi Naradastatha
Asito Devalovyaasaha Svayam Chaiva Braveeshime

After listening to Krishna for so many verses and realising that the one he is talking to is none other than the Supreme Lord (Mahavishnu / Krishna), Arjuna accepts the facts and states – you are the Supreme Lord. He agrees that Krishna is the beginning, HE does not have birth or death. I heard similar statements from Great sages like Narada and Vyasa advocating you as the Supreme Power. Now, I am hearing directly from you. I agree with and trust everything that you have told me thus far.

After listening to those determined messages by Krishna in the last three chapters, now Arjuna is thoroughly convinced and able to be firm from the fluctuating state of mind.

Another trait of a good listener is not just listening but repeat what has been told or informed. This helps retaining the knowledge and register firmly in their minds. The true disciple will listen carefully, understand the essence of the message, and reconfirm what has been learnt.

Just like people give their examinations, organisations perform the knowledge transfer and have a playback session to ensure the knowledge is completely transferred. Similarly, Arjuna summarised what Krishna said in the previous chapters and confirmed his understanding and consensus with the Supreme Lord.

कथं विद्यामहं योगिंस्त्वां सदा परिचिन्तयन् ।
केषु केषु च भावेषु चिन्त्योऽसि भगवन्मया ॥

Katham VidyaamahamYogistwaam Sadaa Parichintayan
Keshu Keshu Cha Bhaaveshu Chintyosi Bhagavanmayaa

After understanding various forms of Krishna, Arjuna is curious about where to find him and asks – please explain where can I see you? How can I recognise you? Explain the forms in which he is living in this material world.

He forgot about the war and the emotions of the battle, but he is evolving to learn more about the ultimate Truth. Assuming the Supreme Lord stands in front of us and has a dialogue with us, it becomes difficult to speak about materialistic things but praise or admire him.

Assuming a situation when we suddenly come across our most admired celebrity, we will not prepare ourselves about what to discuss or what to ask; our first conversation, is to praise them about their past achievements or express how much we like or admire them, and if time permits, we try to understand more about them. Similarly, though Arjuna spent many years with Krishna, he is living in a moment when he is discovering and understanding the ultimate Truth and speaking to the Supreme Lord. Everything else became pointless.

श्रीभगवानुवाच ।

हन्त ते कथयिष्यामि दिव्या ह्यात्मविभूतयः ।

प्राधान्यतः कुरुश्रेष्ठ नास्त्यन्तो विस्तरस्य मे ॥

Hanta Te Kathayishaami Divyaa Hyatmavibhootayaha

Praadhaanyataha Kurusreshtha Naastyantho Vistarasya me

Arjuna, my existence in this material world is limitless or countless. It is very difficult to document everything that I am capable of or my existing in different forms. However, let me provide few examples as a quick reference.

- I am the Supreme Soul in every living being.
- I am the Beginning, Middle and End of them.
- I am Vishnu in the Adityas (Suns). According to the Vedas, there are 12 forms of Aditya, the Sun.
- I am the Sun, in the Brightness (there is nothing brighter than the Sun)
- I am the Marichi in the Saptarishis (One of the greatest sage of Seven Sages born from the mind of Brahma)

- I am the Moon in the stars (There is nothing more beautiful and brighter star than the Moon among the stars. Moon also provides the nectar to the planet to regenerate the energies)
- I am the Samaveda in four Vedas (Rig, Yagur, Sama and Adharvana – Sam Veda is a beautiful song)
- I am the Indra in Devas (King of Devatas)
- I am the mind in the senses (which is the most powerful and controls the five materialistic senses)
- I am the Life in the living beings
- I am the Siva in Rudras (there are 12 Rudras)
- I am the Kubera among Demons and Devatas (Kubera possesses all sources of wealth and prosperity).
- I am the Fire in the Vasus (Astha Vasuvulu – Sky, Earth, Water, Wind, Fire, Stars, Sun and Moon)
- I am Mount Meru in the Mountains. (According to Sanatana Dharma, Mount Meru is at the centre point of the North Pole, from which the Universe's dimensions can be determined)
- I am the Brihaspati in the Ministers (Brihaspati is the Minister for Indira. Him being Indra, as stated earlier, He is the Brihaspati – the key minister or advisor)

- I am the Karthikeya in the Senas (Army) (Army chief of the Devatas – Son of Lord Siva)
- I am the Bhrigu out of the great Maharshis.
- I am the Aum of all the Sounds – The first sound emerged.
- I am the Himalayas in the places – The tallest Mountain in the world.
- I am the chant in the Yagnas (Yagnas are performed through chanting various Vedas. Without chanting Veda, no Yagna can be performed. Directly stating, there is no Yagna without him)
- I am the Banyan tree among the trees – (Biggest tree, which could be difficult to identify the bening, the middle or the end of the tree)
- I am Narada of the Devarishis
- I am the Chitraradha of the Gandharvas
- I am the Sage Kapilamaharshi of all the sages (Vishnu incarnated as Kapila Maharshi to narrate Sankhya Yogam (in-depth knowledge of Chapter 2, that portrays the circle of life, to his Mother and blessed her Moksha – Ultimate peace)
- I am the Uchchaisravam (Divine Horse) born during the churning of the Milky Ocean.

- I am the Iravata in the Elephants (Divine Elephant) born during the churning of the Milky Ocean
- I am the King among human beings
- I am the diamond sword of Indra in the weapons (The sharpest and most potent sword)
- I am the Kamadhenu (Holy Cow) among the cows (Kamadhenu born during the churning of the Milky Ocean)
- I am the Manmadha (Source of Love)
- I am the Vasuki in the serpent (Vasuki is the snake that is associated with Lord Siva)
- I am the Ananta (Countless hooded snake) in the Nagas – Nagas have multiple hoods, while serpents have only one hood. (Sri Maha Vishnu resides on this Ananta in his Yoga Nidra (meditation)
- I am the Rain god among the waters
- I am the Aryama among the forefathers who looks after the well-being of the departed.
- I am the Yama among those who instil righteousness (Yamadharmaraj God of Death who executes balanced punishment for the souls after their lifespan based on their acts during their lifetime. Garuda Puran – a conversation between Lord Vishnu and his chariot Garud (Eagle) provides in-depth information about soul travel after leaving the material world)

- I am the Prahlada among the Demons (Highest ranked disciple of Lord Vishnu among the Demons)
- I am the Time
- I am the Lion among the animals
- I am the Garuda (Eagle) among the birds
- I am the Air in the clean objects
- I am the Rama among perfect Men who instilled righteousness
- I am the Crocodile among the water species
- I am the river Ganga among the rivers (most sacred River)
- I am the Akaram (Alphabet "A") AUM in Sanskrit starts with A U M
- I am the Dwandwa Samasam (Dual Compounds of the compound words)
- I am the Brahma, the Creator of the universe
- I am the Death in the destruction
- Among women, I am the Fame, fortune, kind speech, memory, intelligence, patience, and persistence (the most potent traits of women)
- I am the Brihatsamam in Samavedam
- I am the Gayatri Chandas among the Vedic grammar
- I am Margaseersha among the months

- I am the Vasantaritu (Spring) in the seasons
- I am the Gambling among the Cheating works
- I am the Splendour among the Splendid
- I am the Victory, Adventure, and Strength among the strongest
- I am the Vasudeva in the Vrusni descendants. The clan of Yadu dynasty in which Krishna is born.
- I am Arjuna among the Pandavas

At the beginning of the Universe, Mahabharata History mentions how Nara (the equivalent of Krishna) and Narayana (Krishna) emerged. There is no difference between them. However, Arjuna, taking birth as a great warrior, does not remember the past, but as Krishna said, he is always aware of the past, present, and future.

- I am the Vyasa among great sages
    - *Vyasa is the incarnation of Sri Mahavishnu, and hence, he is also called Vyasa Bhagavan (God). Vyasa descended to the Earth to bifurcate all the Vedas and Upanishads into well-structured Vedas (Rig, Yagur, Sama and Adharvana). He went on to document the Mahabharata, Asthadasa Puranas as the guide principle for humankind on the ways of living. The essence of all the Vedas, Upanishads and Puranas are filtered, summarised and delivered by*

Krishna as Bhagavad Gita to the humankind through Arjuna.

- *Hence, it has gained so much importance in this land of Karma (Duty). Bharata (India) is called Karma Bhoomi, where duties are performed with righteousness and complete devotion to the Supreme Lord. All other lands are meant for pleasure, as stated in the Srimad Bhagavadam.*
- *Since the world is in the Kalyug, righteousness is going through a challenging time and just before the beginning of Kali Yuga, Krishna provided these timeless lessons to the humankind.*

- I am the Sukracharya among the priests (Sukracharya is the most knowledgeable priest among the priests)
- I am the Law Enforcement for those who deviate from the law of nature
- I am the Truth among those who wish for Victory

(Victory can be achieved by Truth or Corruption. A victory by following Truthfulness is righteous victory)

- I am the silent among the secrets

(Imagine the power of silence. How secretive the information can be – Every association of the reference

is so precise and perfect that one should start visualising Krishna in everything that they see)

- I am the Wisdom among the knowledgeable people
- I am the Seed for all the living beings. The Seed which has no end
- There is nothing in this Universe which does not have my presence
- There is no limit to my existence
- This glorious Universe emerged from me, and in summary, I support all of it with a small fragment.

This concludes that anything and everything we see, touch, and feel are his forms.

If we observe Him everywhere, we will not hurt or harm anyone, whether it is a small creature or the most potent enemy.

Chapter 11

Viswaroopam (The Universal Form)

अर्जुन उवाच

मदनुग्रहाय परमं गुह्यमध्यात्मसंज्ञितम् ।

यत्त्वयोक्तं वचस्तेन मोहोऽयं विगतो मम ॥

Mad Anugrahaaya Paramam Guhyam Adhyaatmasamgyitam

Yettvayoktham Vachastena Mohoyam Vigato Mama

After listening to Krishna talk about his different forms of existence, Arjuna admits that all his illusions and hallucinations have been erased.

Oh Krishna, all my illusions are burnt like grasshoppers wandering around the fire.

एवमेतद्यथात्थ त्वमात्मानं परमेश्वर ।
द्रष्टुमिच्छामि ते रूपमैश्वरं पुरुषोत्तम ॥

Evam Etatdythaathya Twam Aatma Atmaanam Parameshwara
Drashtum Ichchaami Te Roopam Ishwaram Purushottama

मन्यसे यदि तच्छक्यं मया द्रष्टुमिति प्रभो ।
योगेश्वर ततो मे त्वं दर्शयात्मानमव्ययम् ॥

Manyase Yadi Tachchkyam Maya Darshtumiti Prabho
Yogeswara Jato Me Twam Darshayaatmaanam Avyayam

After listening to his various forms, presence in multiple objects, and supremacy among the best, Arjuna becomes curious and wants to witness Krishna's universal form and how the greatest of all greats look like. Arjuna now wishes to visualise Krishna's eternal form (Divine Form) only if Krishna believes that he is worthy.

We sometimes find ourselves demanding the fulfilment of desires, regardless of whether we truly deserve them or not. However, only those who are deserving will ultimately achieve their goals. For instance, we encourage our children to earn good scores to be rewarded, or leaders motivate their teams to deliver exceptional performance recognise or reward. In some instances, as an individual, people may believe that they have delivered exceptional performance, however, the perspective at the leadership could be different.

This is why Krishna advised Arjuna to focus on performing his duty detached from the outcome. Since he is facing the battle of righteousness, the result is up to the supreme power to bestow the wishes.

In summary, instead of demanding what we think we deserve, it is wise to let the leaders assess our worthiness. When we align our efforts with this approach, results will naturally follow. Such an approach is challenging in the material world but can be achieved with practice and consistency.

If Arjuna was not capable or the deserving candidate, Krishna might not have chosen him as his disciple to have this invaluable conversation.

श्रीभगवानुवाच ।

पश्य मे पार्थ रूपाणि शतशोऽथ सहस्रशः ।

नानाविधानि दिव्यानि नानावर्णाकृतीनि च ॥

Sri Bhagavan Uvacha

Pashya Me Paartha Roopaani Ssatasotha Sahasrasaha

Nanavidhaani Divyaani Naanaa Varnaakrutini Cha

Krishna speaks – Arjuna witness the Twelve Suns, Vasus, Twelve Rudras, Saptarishis and others. Similarly, witness the incredible view that no one had ever seen before you. It is not possible to witness everything you have heard so far with your naked eyes. Let me bestow divine vision for you to visualise my universal form.

From here on, Krishna displays his Universal form to Arjuna.

सञ्जय उवाच ।

Sanjaya describes the wonders that Arjuna is witnessing. Please refer to the preface, where I mentioned that Vedavyasa offered Sanjaya a Divine Vision.

Sanjaya Uvacha

एवमुक्त्वा ततो राजन्महायोगेश्वरो हरिः ।

दर्शयामास पार्थाय परमं रूपमैश्वरम् ॥

Evamuktvaa Tato Rajan Mahayogeswaro Harihi

Darsayamaasa Paarthaaya Paramam Roopamaisvaram

Sanjaya continues to narrate, "By saying so, O King (Dhritarashtra), Supreme Yogi, Sri Maha Vishu, Krishna provided divine vision to Arjuna to witness his Universal Form". And Aruna witnesses –

अनेकवक्त्रनयनमनेकाद्भुतदर्शनम् ।
अनेकदिव्याभरणं दिव्यानेकोद्यतायुधम् ॥

Anekavaktranayanam Anaekaadbhuta Darsanam
Anekadivyaabharanam Divyaanokodyataayudham

दिव्यमाल्याम्बरधरं दिव्यगन्धानुलेपनम् ।
सर्वाश्चर्यमयं देवमनन्तं विश्वतोमुखम् ॥

Divyamaalaambaradharam Divyagandhaanulepanam
Sarwascharyamayam Devam Anantam Vsiwatomukham

Countless eyes, mouths, indescribable views of the galaxy, celestial jewellery, garlands, scents, splendorous view of the universal form. He witnessed as if the thousands of the suns appeared at once in the sky.

Observing such divine supreme power, amazed and surprised Arjuna bowed himself towards HIM and prayed to him.

Oh, Krishna, I can witness all the divine gods, living beings, the Brahma, Shiva, Sages, and divine snakes. I can also witness countless shoulders, stomachs, faces, eyes, etc. I cannot see your beginning, middle or the end. I see you everywhere.

किरीटिनं गदिनं चक्रिणं च

तेजोराशिं सर्वतो दीप्तिमन्तम् ।

पश्यामि त्वां दुर्निरीक्ष्यं समन्ताद्

दीप्तानलार्कद्युतिमप्रमेयम्

Kireetinam Gadinam Chakrinam cha Tejoraasim Sarvato Deeptamantam

Pasyami Twaam Durnireekshayam Samantaad Deeptaanalaarkadyutimaprameyam

I am unable to see you through the enormous light as if it is emerging from thousands of Suns. While I could barely visualise, I observe many divine crowns, maces, and wheels (Sudarshana Chakra). I am certain now that You are the first ever divine power. You are the supporter of the entire Universe. You are forever. The Sun and Moon are your eyes. All the living beings across different planets are shivering, looking at your horrifying form. The demigods enter you while paying respects, and a few people pray with fear. At the same time, great sages and divine people are praising you by chanting Vedas with pleasant minds.

You love and hate him, but you cannot ignore him. He is the ultimate Truth, and everyone must return to him. Those who realise this and recognise him as the ultimate Truth or Lord Vishnu are comfortable, while others are not.

There are a couple of hidden secrets I would like to highlight. On one side, as Arjuna observed, some are terrified and shivering, while others look at the same form with a pleasant mind and pay respects to the Universal Form. How can one person find it horrifying while another finds it pleasant? It is important to note that living fearlessly is possible by following Dharma. Those who engage in demonic deeds naturally fear being exposed and punished for their actions. We can observe the same thing in real life. If we live honestly, we don't have to worry about the law, whereas the lawbreakers always live in fear.

On the other hand, Arjuna mentions about the living beings from different planets. The likes of Pitru Devas, the Serpents, the Demigods, etc., each have their respective planets.

The concept of life beyond Earth was established thousands of years ago. It is just that no one can visualise them with biological eyes.

Arjuna continues, I see multiple forms of Shiva, Suns, Vasus, Saints, Demigods, Pitru Devtas (demigods of the forefathers), Gandharvas (Divine kings), Yakshas, Demnos (Rakshasas), and scholars are looking at you with shock.

Looking at such a form, all the living beings across the planets are scared, and along with them, I am, too. I am shivering and shocked to see the face resembling death, Burning like fire, with large, sharp and horrifying teeth. Similar to that the rivers flow towards the seas, I can observe the kings of Pandava's side and the sons of

Dhritarastra, Bheeshma, Drona, Karna and many more great warriors rushing towards your horrific face. Few struck to your sharp teeth with crushed faces. I can also observe that you are swallowing them away from all directions as they fall into your blazing face. I am unable to recognise you in this form. Please be gracious to me and calm down. Please help me understand who you are, as it is challenging to see the universal form.

श्रीभगवानुवाच ।

कालोऽस्मि लोकक्षयकृत्प्रवृद्धो

लोकान्समाहर्तुमिह प्रवृत्तः ।

ऋतेऽपि त्वां न भविष्यन्ति सर्वे

येऽवस्थिताः प्रत्यनीकेषु योधाः ॥

Sri Bhagavan Uvacha

Kaalo Asmin Lokakshayakrutpravrudhdho

Lokaansamaahartumiha Pravruktaha

Srotepi Twaam Na Bhavishanti Sarve Yevasthitaaha Pratyaneekeshu Yodhaaha

Krishna says, "O Arjuna, I am the indestructible time. I am the destroyer of the world. I came to this world to kill all these people who are not living with righteousness. Even if you don't fight the battle, they will be destroyed by me. Hence, Arjuna, do not hesitate. Pick up your armoury. This is a lifetime opportunity to fight for righteousness, and the doors of the heavens will be opened for you with open arms. You are just doing your job. Drona, Bheeshma, Jayadhradha, Karna and many other warriors were already killed by me. Hence, do not be worried and do your duty. You will undoubtedly win the war".

Arjuna says, "O Krishna, it is quite obvious that the great sages and scholars are worshipping you and praying to you while the demons are trying to shatter and run away from you with fear."

त्वमादिदेवः पुरुषः पुराण-

स्त्वमस्य विश्वस्य परं निधानम्।

वेत्तासि वेद्यं च परं च धाम

त्वया ततं विश्वमनन्तरूप॥

Twamaadidevaha Purushha Puraanastwamasya
Vishvasya Param Nidhaanam

Vettasi Vedyam Cha Param Cha Dhaama Twayaa Tatam
Visvvamanantaroopam

You are superior to the Lord Brahma - the Creator. How will they not respect you? You are the ultimate Truth, which does not have limits. You are the reason for everything. I now realise you are this Universe's oldest, first-ever form.

सखेति मत्वा प्रसभं यदुक्तं
हे कृष्ण हे यादव हे सखेति ।
अजानता महिमानं तवेदं
मया प्रमादात्प्रणयेन वापि ॥

Sakheti Matvaa Prasabham Yaduktam, Hey Krishna Hey Yaadava, Hey Sakheti
Ajaanataa Mahimaanam Tavedam Mayaa Pramaadaatpranayena vaapi

यच्चावहासार्थमसत्कृतोऽसि
विहारशय्यासनभोजनेषु ।
एकोऽथवाप्यच्युत तत्समक्षं
तत्क्षामये त्वामहमप्रमेयम् ॥

Yachchavahaasaarthamasatkruto asi
Vihaarasayyasanabhojaneshu
Ekothavaapyachyuta Tasmam Ksham Tatkshamaye Tvam Ahamaptrameyam

Oh, Krishna, please forgive me. I wittingly addressed you as Hey Krishna, Hey Yadava, Oh Friend, and in many other ways. I made fun of you while travelling, eating, or playing, assuming you were like anyone among us.

It is unimaginable if the greatest of the great (the Lord) comes and stands in front of us, calling them by name and playfully joking with them. Arjuna experiences the similar emotion, realising that Krishna is none other than the Supreme Lord Mahavishnu. Reacting to how he addressed him on different occasions in the past, he felt ashamed and requested forgiveness.

Despite being greatest warrior, Arjuna remained humble without any pride of his accomplishments and pleading for forgiveness from the Lord Krishna. The character of Arjuna teaches the humanity to be grounded and being humble irrespective of their accomplishments instead of showing arrogance and pride that he or she is the reason for all the success.

अदृष्टपूर्वं हृषितोऽस्मि दृष्ट्वा

भयेन च प्रव्यथितं मनो मे ।

तदेव मे दर्शय देव रूपं

प्रसीद देवेश जगन्निवास ॥

Ahrasruporrvam Hrushitosmi Hrushtvaa Bhayena Pravyathitam Mano Me

Tadeva me Darshsya Deva Roopam Praseeda Devesa Jagannivasa

With tearful eyes and sense of guilt for addressing Krishna inappropriately, he pleads for forgiveness. Arjuna requests Krishna to withdraw his universal form and reveal his simple divine form.

किरीटिनं गदिनं चक्रहस्तं

इच्छामि त्वां द्रष्टुमहं तथैव ।

तेनैव रूपेण चतुर्भुजेन

सहस्रबाहो भव विश्वमूर्ते ॥

Kireetinam Gadinam Chakrahastham Ichchaami Tvaam Drastumaham Tathyiva

Teniva Rupena Caturbhujena Sahasrabaaho Bhava Viswamurte

If you are considerate, I would like to see your simple form of wearing the crown, mace, and divine wheel (Sudarsana Chakra) and holding them with your four arms.

श्रीभगवानुवाच ।

मया प्रसन्नेन तवार्जुनेदं

रूपं परं दर्शितमात्मयोगात् ।

तेजोमयं विश्वमनन्तमाद्यं

यन्मे त्वदन्येन न दृष्टपूर्वम् ॥

Maya Prasannena Tavaarjunedam Rupam Param Darsitamaatmayogaat

Tejomayam Viswamanantamaadhyam Yanme Tvadanyena na Hrusrupoorvam

न वेदयज्ञाध्ययनैर्न दानै-

र्न च क्रियाभिर्न तपोभिरुग्रैः ।

एवंरूपः शक्य अहं नृलोके

द्रष्टुं त्वदन्येन कुरुप्रवीर ॥

Na vedayagynadhyananairna daanou rna cha kriyaabhirna Tapobhirugrou

Yevamrupaha Saskya Aham Nruloke Drasthum Tvadnyena Kurupraveera

Arjuna, out of my own will, I demonstrated my universal form to you. Such form was never seen by anyone before you. Even if someone performs intense penance, sacrifice, and prayers, it is almost unlikely to witness such a form of mine.

I now free you from such scary universal form and bring my pleasant form in front of you as you wished for. By saying so, Krishna withdrew his universal form and transformed himself into a simple form of Lord Vishnu, as Arjuna requested.

अर्जुन उवाच ।

दृष्ट्वेदं मानुषं रूपं तव सौम्यं जनार्दन ।

इदानीमस्मि संवृत्तः सचेताः प्रकृतिं गतः ॥

Arjuna Uvacha

Hrustvedam Maanusham Roopam Tava Soumyam Janaardana

Idaanemasmi Samvruttaha Sachetaaha Prakrutim Gataha

After witnessing the pleasant form, Arjuna says - Oh, Janardhana, now I feel so pleasant after looking at your beautiful human form, and my Mind has regained its peace.

(Janardhana – the man who uplifts the mankind – look at the names Krishna is referred to as. He is uplifting Arjuna and through him, the Humankind).

श्रीभगवानुवाच ।

सुदुर्दर्शमिदं रूपं दृष्टवानसि यन्मम ।

देवा अप्यस्य रूपस्य नित्यं दर्शनकाङ्क्षिणः ॥

Sri Bhagavan Uvacha

Sudurdarsamidam Roopam Hrustruvaanasi Yanmama

Devaa Apyasya Roopasya Nityam Darsanakaankshinaha

This is my rare form, and even the gods and demigods perform deep penance to see such a form of mine.

Those who think about me, who keep me in their minds all the time, will always reach me.

Chapter 12

Bhakti Yogam (Love towards the Eternal)

अर्जुन उवाच

एवं सततयुक्ता ये भक्तास्त्वां पर्युपासते ।

ये चाप्यक्षरमव्यक्तं तेषां के योगवित्तमाः ॥

Arjuna Uvacha

Evam Satatayuktaa Yo Bhaktaastvaam Paryupaasate

Ye chaapyaksharam vaktam Teshaam Ke Yogavittamaaha.

After witnessing the indescribable universal and pleasant forms, Arjuna wants to understand, according to Krishna, who is considered a complete devotee. Those who worship a physical or unlimited universal form are considered complete devotees.

श्रीभगवानुवाच ।

मय्यावेश्य मनो ये मां नित्ययुक्ता उपासते ।

श्रद्धया परयोपेताः ते मे युक्ततमा मताः ॥

Sri Bhagavan Uvacha

Mayaaveshya Mano Ye Maam Nityayuktaa Upaasate

Sraddhayaa Parayopetaaha Te Me Yuktatamaa Mataaha

ये त्वक्षरमनिर्देश्यमव्यक्तं पर्युपासते ।

सर्वत्रगमचिन्त्यञ्च कूटस्थमचलन्ध्रुवम् ॥

Ye Tvaksharam Indreshyam vaktam paryupaasate

Sarvatra Jamachintyanam cha Kootasthamchalam Dhruvam

Physical form worshipers are dear to me. The path towards worshipping my unmanifested form or unlimited form is challenging. However, in the end, both will attain my supreme abode.

It is quite difficult and challenging to concentrate on universal or unmanifested form. Hence it is fine to be devoted to the physical form. It is easier to concentrate on physical appearance compared to unmanifested.

People might question how humankind can know how Krishna, Shiva, Brahma or any other Godheads look like they have been portrayed. The great Rishis or Sages performed intense penance, visualised the Godheads and described in the Vedic scriptures the way they witnessed God with their divine eye similar to that of the Viswaroopa Darshanam (previous chapter); Arjuna described Krishna with (Kireetinam, Gadinam, Chakrinam...) wearing a Crown, holding Mace, Sudarsana Chakra and the lotus.

In this chapter, Krishna suggested ways for humankind to devote themselves to Him.

Control all the senses and concentrate entirely upon ME to reach my supreme abode. If that is difficult, then perform the prayers as prescribed. If people consider that very difficult, performing the duties devoted to Krishna will also help people attain the supreme abode. Assuming that is also not possible, sacrifice the results of your duties. Even if that is impossible, at least try to spread the knowledge. Prayers are superior to spreading knowledge.

Krishna suggested a chronological order of the rituals one should try to follow to attain supreme abode. Firstly, he suggested the most difficult path: controlling his Mind and devoting himself to him. In the end, he suggested spreading knowledge about HIM. The most straightforward way to reach him. Had he told the most straightforward way first, humankind would never have taken the challenging path.

The journey to significant achievements often begins with simple steps. By often participating in conversations and sharing knowledge about HIM will lead to deeper understanding about HIM. Consistent daily devotion helps us perform duties without desires. As people detach from desires, it becomes easier to control the mind, ultimately guiding humankind to HIS supreme abode.

Selfless people who do not get influenced by let external factors to be happy or sad, do not get anxious, treat everyone equally, and have a balanced mind are dear to ME.

Sanatana Dharma advocates being free from greed, anger, and selfishness and treating everyone equally. At the same time, take the steps towards understanding the eternal bliss to reach HIM in the end. The conversation in Sanatana Dharma is not about how happily people live in this materialistic world, but it is about achieving the heavenly abode and never returning back which leads to stay away from the lotus feet of Lord Vishnu (Supreme Power).

Chapter 13

Prakriti Purushudu, Chaitanyam (Nature, Enjoyer and Consciousness)

अर्जुन उवाच ।

प्रकृतिं पुरुषं चैव क्षेत्रं क्षेत्रज्ञमेव च ।

एतद्वेदितुमिच्छामि ज्ञानं ज्ञेयं च केशव ॥

Arjuna Uvacha

Prakrutim Purusham Chaiva Kshetra
Kshetragyameva Cha

Etadveditumichchaami Gyanam Gneyam Cha Kesava

Arjuna is trying to understand the difference between Nature and the Person, the difference between the Physical Body (Kshetra) and the Soul (Kshetragnya). The Soul resides in body; for the Soul, the body is the Kshetra.

The very first verses of Bhagavad Gita are Dharma Kshetre and Kuru Kshetre. Our body can be referred to as Kurukshetra, where a battle of dilemmas occurs every time between right (Dharma) and wrong (Adharma). Those Kshetras (bodies) that perform righteousness all the time will always be the Dharma Kshetras. Arjuna wants to differentiate between the physical body and the Soul and the wisdom that can be achieved.

Clarity around these will help humankind relate to every activity they perform.

श्रीभगवानुवाच ।

इदं शरीरं कौन्तेय क्षेत्रमित्यभिधीयते ।

एतद्यो वेत्ति तं प्राहुः क्षेत्रज्ञ इति तद्विदः ॥

Sri Bhagavan Uvacha

Idam Sareeram Kaunteya Kshetramityabhidheeyate

Etadyo Vetthi Tam Praahuhu Kshetragyna Iti Tadvidaha

क्षेत्रज्ञं चापि मां विद्धि सर्वक्षेत्रेषु भारत ।

क्षेत्रक्षेत्रज्ञयोर्ज्ञानं यत्तज्ज्ञानं मतं मम ॥

Kshetragynam Chaapi Maam Vidhdhi Sarvakshetreshu Bharata

KshetraKshetragynaanam Yat Gyanam Matam Mama

Kshetra is nothing but the physical living body. It is not just the human body; it can be the body of an animal or a worm. Kshetragyna is referred to as the Supreme Soul. He exists in every living being as a Supreme Soul. After realising that Krishna is everywhere, people will never discriminate.

Now, even if we look at the minutest worm, it contains a body (Kshetra) and a Supreme Soul (Kshetragyna). That's how the Sanatana Dharma identified every living or non-living being as HIS form. The tradition of Sanatana Dharma can be observed: people greet one another with folded hands and touch the feet of elders, gurus, and scholars. Such respects are paid to the Supreme Soul (Kshetragyna), which resides in the physical body (Kshetra). Those who understand this will treat everyone equally.

Those who can understand the five supreme elements (Earth, sky, water, air and fire), illusion, arrogance, and Mind, the ten elements that control the human Mind - ears, nose, eyes, tongue and skin help to attain knowledge. Voice, Legs, Hands, Anus and Genitals are the working elements. Adding Mind to it will become eleven. Then, there are five objects of sense: smell, taste, form, touch, and sound. The entire human body operates with above twenty-four elements.

There is no doubt that the above twenty-four elements that control the human body are the cause of materialistic happiness or sadness.

Obedience, humility, nonviolence *(non-violence should not be misunderstood as merely refraining from physical harm. Causing emotional pain to others should also be considered as act of violence. Try to practice nonviolence)*, tolerance, simplicity, seeking guidance through scholarly teachers (Gurus), self-control, differentiating between life and death, detachment from the families and friends, trust and devotion towards the Lord Vishnu, interest towards the divine knowledge are the key elements of the knowledge and wisdom.

People can ask, if one needs to be detached from all emotions and desires, then what is the point of fighting the battle, and why is Krishna suggesting Arjuna fight the battle? If everyone is treated equally and people respect each other by sharing, donating, and thinking about the supreme Lord, there is no hatred, no vengeance, no cross-border tensions, and no poor or rich. Imagine such a beautiful and happy world. Krishna's objective is to instil the righteousness and law of nature.

As Krishna said, when dishonesty and cheating rule over righteousness, at every stage of the Yuga, Krishna will take birth to bring the balance back. Krishna suggests how to mould our lives to attain the heavens (live peacefully). The initial chapters also indicated that one should perform one's duty to achieve that heavenly abode.

Performing the duty without any desires or attachments, devoting to the Supreme Soul (Krishna), and Praying to him in different ways will help the Soul reach the Heavenly abode.

यथा प्रकाशयत्येकः कृत्स्नं लोकमिमं रविः ।
क्षेत्रं क्षेत्री तथा कृत्स्नं प्रकाशयति भारत ॥

Yathaa Prakaashayateykaha Krutsnam
Kokamimam Ravihi
Kshetram Kshetre Tatha Krutsnam
Prakaasayati Bhaarata

Dear Arjuna, just like the Sun illuminates this Universe and spreads all over, the Soul is spread across the human body.

As stated in Narayana Sukta,

Padmakosa Pratikasagm Hridayam Chapyathomukham,
Atho Nistya Vitasyante Nabhamupari Tisthati

Tasya sikhaya made Paramatma vyavasthitaha.
Sa Brahma Sa Sivaha Sa Harihi Sendra Soksharah
Paramaswarat.

The slokas (verses) describe the exact location of the Supreme soul in our body. The Supreme Soul resides above the navel of every human being, in the form of a small flame in the middle of a lotus flower. That flame is nothing but the Brahma, the Vishnu, the Siva, the Indra, and the Akshara (Letter AUM), the Supreme Power.

The Vedic texts provide the exact location of a human being's life (not in the heart that beats, which is another muscle doing its duty). Once the flame stops illuminating, that's the moment the Soul leaves the body, and the heart stops beating. The flame in space (the Sun in the Universe) and the flame inside the human body in minute form are the same. Like the Sun, the flame retains consciousness within the human body.

Those who can utilise the knowledge and wisdom to understand the difference between the Human Body, The Soul, and The Supreme Soul will reach the heavenly abode and are dear to Krishna.

Chapter 14

Prakriti Triguna (Three Characteristics of the Nature)

श्रीभगवानुवाच

मम योनिर्महद् ब्रह्म तस्मिन्गर्भं दधाम्यहम् ।

सम्भवः सर्वभूतानां ततो भवति भारत ॥

Sri Bhagavan Uvacha

MamaYonirmahad Brahma Tatsmingarbham Dadhaamyaham

Smbhavaha Sarvabhootaanaam Tato Bhavati Bharata

Now, Krishna explains the characteristics of nature.

Brahma the Creator of this Universe emerged out of Lord Vishnu (Krishna). He is the primary seed of everything that we witness. Human beings wander between Satva Rajo and Tamo gunas.

Satva determines the pleasant and happiness.

Rajo determines the desires and lust.

Tamo determines the anger, Ignorance, etc.

Out of the three, Satva Guna (Character) is better. Rajo Guna leads to the vicious circle of life, while Tamo Guna leads to hell.

We often observe those who lose their temper and become very angry. They become ignorant of their surroundings and utter profound offensive statements or commit sins.

Those who are pleasant and happy will have the opportunity to improve their wisdom and attempt to know the Supreme Soul.

Each living being reacts differently at different stages influenced by these three characteristics. Those who rise above the three characteristics will migrate to the heavenly abode and reach the Supreme Soul.

अर्जुन उवाच।

कैर्लिङ्गैस्त्रीन्गुणानेतानतीतो भवति प्रभो।

किमाचारः कथं चैतांस्त्रीन्गुणानतिवर्तते॥

Arjuna Uvacha

Kair Lingestreen Gunaanetaanateeto Bhavati Prabho

Kimaachaaraha Katham Chitaamstreen Kunaanativartate

How do we recognise a person beyond nature's three characteristics? How will he behave, or how does someone disconnect from these elements?

Krishna explains –

- Those who will not feel pride, detached from the dual facet pleasures such as success or failure,
- Those who treat everyone equally treat the sand, stone and gold equally,
- Those who treat happiness and sadness as the same (The living examples are great sages like, Jagadguru Adi Shankaracharya, Kanchi Kamakoti peetadhipati Chandramoulishwara, Bharati Teerdha Swami from Sringeri Saradapeetham, Bhagavan Ramana Maharshi, Bheemly Shivanandam garu and many others).

Such saintly people are completely detached from worldly desires. They spread awareness of divine wisdom and show the path towards ultimate happiness.

In simple words, Krishna says, all the materialistic emotions are short living things. Hence, suggests that you rise above and lead a pleasant life.

धर्मसंस्थापनाथामय सम्भवामर् युगे युगे

Is it possible in this materialistic world? Again, As Krishna said earlier, consistency and practice make it possible.

ब्रह्मणो हि प्रतिष्ठाहममृतस्याव्ययस्य च ।

शाश्वतस्य च धर्मस्य सुखस्यैकान्तिकस्य च ॥

Brahmano Hi Prathisthaha Aham
Amrutasyaavyarasya Cha
Saaswatasya Dharmasya Sukhasaikaantikasya Cha

Sri Krishna is declaring himself: I am the Nectar, I am forever, I am the final destiny, and I am the ultimate happiness. I am the source of everything.

Chapter 15
Purushottama Yogam (The Supreme Person)

श्रीभगवानुवाच ।

ऊर्ध्वमूलमधःशाखमश्वत्थं प्राहुरव्ययम् ।

छन्दांसि यस्य पर्णानि यस्तं वेद स वेदवित् ॥

Sri Bhagavan Uvacha

Urdhvamoolam Adhaha Saakhamakshvaththam Praahuravyayam

Chandaamsi Yasya Parnaani Yastam Veda Sa Vedavit

Comparing human life with the oldest Banyan tree, the roots are like the desires of living beings. Those who detach themselves from these roots will rise and realise the ultimate Truth.

न तद्भासयते सूर्यो न शशाङ्को न पावकः ।

यद्गत्वा न निवर्तन्ते तद्धाम परमं मम ॥

धर्मसंस्थापनाथामय सम्भवामर् युगे युगे

Na Tat Abhyaasayate Suryo Na Sashaangnye na Paavakaha

Yadgatwa Na Nivarthante Tadhaama Paramam Mama

For those who practice detachment from roots of desires, will reach my supreme abode, such an abode is not illuminated by the Sun, The Moon or the Fire.

The abode where Lord Vishnu (Krishna) resides is so far that even light emerging from the Sun, moon, or fire cannot reach it.

In modern scientific knowledge, scientists speak about the blackhole, which is very far and impossible for humankind to travel physically. Even if someone goes there and returns to the Earth, some millions of years might have elapsed (Time dilation).

In the Mahabharata, the location of Supreme Abode is mentioned.

On one such occasion, Krishna takes Arjuna on an interstellar voyage to show him HIS supreme abode. Such acts prove Krishna to be the Supreme Lord. After a long journey that Krishna and Arjuna pass through a darkest location (which could be the Blackhole). Krishna uses his Sudarshana Chakra to illuminate the darkness passing through. After crossing the dark area, Arjuna witnessed the brightest light possible: where Lord Vishnu in Yoga Nidra (Sleeping) on the Adisesha (countless-headed snake) and his concert goddess Lakshmi beside him.

The Indian Vedic scriptures specified some wonderful and miraculous locations or places a normal human cannot witness with the naked eye. They are only possible through devotion, meditation, and trust in Him. In the materialistic world, human beings look for documentary evidences to believe. For example, after people travelled to different planets, realised there is a time dilation between the planets which was mentioned thousands of years ago in Vedas.

As mentioned earlier, living beings in the materialistic world are attached to the five senses and the sixth one, the Mind. Just like fragrance is carried from one place to another, the Soul travels from one body to another. People will not be able to understand this transformation, but those who obtain the divine third eye (which is possible only through meditation) can. Sages who conquered the Soul were able to visualise such transformations.

गामाविश्य च भूतानि धारयाम्यहमोजसा ।

पुष्णामि चौषधीः सर्वाः सोमो भूत्वा रसात्मकः ॥

Gaamaavishya Cha Bhootaani Dhaarayaamyahamojasaa

Pushnaami Choushadheehi Sarvaaha Somo Bhootvaa Rasaatmakaha

I dwell the required powers in the Sun, the Moon, and the Fire. I exist in every planet. I control the planets' rotation within their orbits without deviation.

Being the moon, He helps plants get vegetation.

Being the fire, he resides in every living being and helps to digest the food consumed.

While digesting spicy food, we sometimes feel burning sensation in our stomach. Our body generates the required digestive enzymes, nothing but enough energy to digest such food. He helps generate the energy needed in the form of acids (Fire) to digest food.

सर्वस्य चाहं हृदि सन्निविष्टो

मत्तः स्मृतिर्ज्ञानमपोहनञ्च ।

वेदैश्च सर्वैरहमेव वेद्यो

वेदान्तकृद्वेदविदेव चाहम् ॥

Sarvasya Cha Aham Hrudai Sannivishto Mattaha Samrutigyaanamapohancha

Vediascha Sarverahameva Vedhyo
Vedaantakrudvedavideva Cha Aham

Is it only humans or animals? No, even plants absorb water and acquire nutrients from the soil. They also go through the digestive process. Such observation establishes His existence everywhere. All the Vedas were scripted by Himself (Krishna).

According to the scriptures, Vedavyasa Maharshi (Sage Vedavyasa - the incarnation of Lord Vishnu) bifurcated all the Vedas and Upanishads into four different partitions (Rig, Yajur, Sama, and Adharvana Vedas). Vedavyasa is also called Vyasa Bhagavan (Vedavyaso Bhagavan Rishihi) and is referred to as the Supreme God.

There are two main types of living beings in this material world: one who is attached to the circle of life and the other who tries to understand the Soul and devotes himself to realising the supreme Soul.

However, there is another person beyond the two, who is veiled across the planets and all living beings. That person is none other than the Supreme Person (Sri Krishna).

यो मामेवमसम्मूढो जानाति पुरुषोत्तमम् ।
स सर्वविद्भजति मां सर्वभावेन भारत ॥

Ye Maamevamasammoodho Jaanaati Purushottamam
Sa Sarvavidbhajati Maam Sarva Bhaavena Bhaarata

Hence, dear Arjuna, trust me and consider me as the Supreme Power without any doubts. Devote yourself to me, and you will win in all your endeavours.

Chapter 16

Daivasura Swabhavam (Characteristics of devotees and demons)

अभयं सत्त्वसंशुद्धिर्ज्ञानयोगव्यवस्थितिः ।

दानं दमश्च यज्ञश्च स्वाध्यायस्तप आर्जवम् ॥

Abhayam Satvasamsudhdhirgyanayogavyavasthitihi

Daanam Damscha Yagnyascha Svaadhyaayastapa Aarjvam

अहिंसा सत्यमक्रोधस्त्यागः शान्तिरपैशुनम् ।

दया भूतेष्वलोलुप्त्वं मार्दवं ह्रीरचापलम् ॥

Ahimsaa Satyamakrodhastyaagaha Saantiraousunam

Dayaa Bhootoshvaloluptvam Maardavam Hreerachaapalam

तेजः क्षमा धृतिः शौचमद्रोहो नातिमानिता ।
भवन्ति सम्पदं दैवीमभिजातस्य भारत ॥

Tejaha Kshamaa Dhrutihi Sochamadroho Naatimaanitaa
Bhavanti Sampaadm Daiveemabhijaatasya Bharata

Understanding the characteristics and behaviours of Saintly and diabolic people.

Those who are fearless, clean, devotional, sacrificing, donate for the right cause, softspoken, nonviolent, pleasant, merciful towards people, and without envy such people are referred to as Saints.

Those who cannot differentiate between right and wrong are envious; possess false prestige, arrogance, and are untidy liars. Those who do not understand the meaning of righteousness are known as sinister. They consider the Universe accurate, believe there is no foundation, and are established based on sex and lust. Lust and greed can never be satisfied. Such diabolical people will never be able to realise the ultimate Soul.

Hence, Arjuna do not shed tears since you are born with reverent characteristics.

इदमद्य मया लब्धमिमं प्राप्स्ये मनोरथम् ।

इदमस्तीदमपि मे भविष्यति पुनर्धनम् ॥

Iadamadya Mayaa Labdhamimam Praapsyo Manoratham

Idamasteedamapi Me Bhavisyati Punardanam

असौ मया हतः शत्रुर्हनिष्ये चापरानपि ।

ईश्वरोऽहमहं भोगी सिद्धोऽहं बलवान्सुखी ॥

Asou Mayaa Hataha Satrurhanishye Chaparaanapi

Eeswarohamaham Bhogee Siddhoham Balavaansukhee

आढ्योऽभिजनवानस्मि कोऽन्योऽस्ति सदृशो मया ।

यक्ष्ये दास्यामि मोदिष्य इत्यज्ञानविमोहिताः ॥

Aadhyobhijanavaanasmi Konyosti Sadruso may

Yaksye Daasyaami Modishya Ityagnyaanavimohitaaha

People with sinister mindsets who continue to acquire money for themselves, even by cheating, assuming everything belongs to themselves, are unable to overcome Lust, Desires and Greed. Krishna hates such people, and He has killed such people in the past and will kill them in the future as well.

Those who do not follow the guiding principles prescribed in the Vedas will not be able to attain heavenly abode.

Those who possess reverent characteristics will eventually reach HIM. In contrast, others are caught in the vicious circle of life, taking innumerable births on Earth and facing life's struggles.

Chapter 17

Sradhatraya Vibhagam (Characteristics of Conviction)

अर्जुन उवाच ।

ये शास्त्रविधिमुत्सृज्य यजन्ते श्रद्धयान्विताः ।

तेषां निष्ठा तु का कृष्ण सत्त्वमाहो रजस्तमः ॥

Arjuna Uvacha

Ye Shaastravethim Utsrujya Yajante Sradhdhayaanvitaaha

Teshaam Nishthaa TuKaa Krishna Satvamaayo Rajastamaha

What happens to the people who practices rituals regularly however, may not follow the prescribed Vedic methods. They fall under which category of Satva, Rajas or Tamo guna?

Krishna divided everything into three main characters (Gunas).

Day-to-day activities performed	Satva Guna	Rajo Guna	Tamo Guna
Follow regular practices	Pray to Gods / Demigods	Live with Desires and Lust	Anger, Ignorance
Eating Habits	Simple, what is relevant and required that provides required nutrition to maintain the human body.	Too much bitter, salty, sour, spicy, or dried food generates much heat in the stomach.	The food that is cooked for more than three hours, tasteless, spoilt or Leftovers
Performing Yagnas (Ritual sacrifices)	For righteousness, consciousness towards the Supreme Lord	To fulfil materialistic desires	Without any interest or devotion, it does not include offerings or donations, and there are no Vedic Chants. Doing it for the namesake
Respects,	Supreme God,	Wants	Those who

Devotes and Prays	Brahmins, Vedic teachers, respect parents, cleanliness, softspoken, away from lust and sex, and nonviolence are associated with the **physical body**. Speaking Truth, loving conversation, and chanting Vedas are associated with the **voice**. Satisfaction, pleasantness, Silence, and self-control are associated with the **Mind**.	respect in society, accepting rewards and appreciation with pride, awarding oneself.	hurt others or hurt themselves
Rewards and recognition	Perform their duties without attachment to the outcomes and avoid worldly desires.	Expect rewards and recognition in return.	Donating to untidy and inappropriate people or donating without respect or devotion

Any duty (Penance, Donation, or prayers) performed with a consciousness toward the Lord and detached from Lust, Anger, and Ignorance is the proper duty and will help one attain heavenly abode. Any other duty will not benefit their current or upcoming lives, and they will remain stuck in this materialistic world.

The verses in this chapter discussed healthy eating habits, spending money wisely and for the right cause (not on unworthy people or organisations that promote anti-social elements), and staying away from worldly desires. These characteristics are not specific to Sanatana Dharma; they are meant for entire humankind to keep minds and souls pure and live pleasant lives.

Chapter 18

Sanyasam (Final Surrender)

अर्जुन उवाच।

संन्यासस्य महाबाहो तत्त्वमिच्छामि वेदितुम्।

त्यागस्य च हृषीकेश पृथक्केशिनिषूदन॥

Arjuna Uvacha

Sanyasasya Mahabaho Tatvamichchaami Veditum

Tyagasya Cha Hrusheekesha Pruthakkoshinishudana

Ultimately, Arjuna wanted to understand the benefits of sacrifice and living with reverence.

श्रीभगवानुवाच।

काम्यानां कर्मणां न्यासं संन्यासं कवयो विदुः।

सर्वकर्मफलत्यागं प्राहुस्त्यागं विचक्षणाः॥

Sri Bhagavan Uvacha

Kaamyaanaam Karmanaam Nyaasam Sanyaasam Kavayo Vidhuhu

Sarvakarmaphalatyaagam Prahustyaagam Vichakshanaaha

Krishna provides a comprehensive summary of his teachings in the last seventeen chapters to conclude. He also clearly indicates the immediate course of action for Humankind.

The definition of a saint is to detach from desires. Detaching from the results of actions is referred to as sacrifice.

Duties such as Yagna (Sacrifice), Dana (Donation), and Tapas (Penance) must never be ignored. Any duty detached from the outcomes is the actual duty.

Those attached to the materialistic desires will permanently be connected to the dual facet emotions (outcomes). Such outcomes are all temporary in nature. Hence, one should rise beyond those and perform their duties passionately towards the Supreme Soul.

Ignorant people assume that not sacrificing regular duties is a sin that controls humankind's rotation in the circle of life. However, Yagna, Dana, and Tapas are some duties that should never be ignored. Such responsibilities should be performed without any attachments or desires.

Krishna then explains the characteristics or behaviours of people possessing Satva Rajas Tamo Gunas. This explanation will help us understand the character and the psychology of the individuals that we interact with:

	Satva	**Rajo**	**Tamo**
Basic traits	Those not impacted by pleasant or unpleasant situations are determined and not influenced by external factors. Those who do not differentiate across different living beings and treat everyone as the same	Differentiating creatures and living beings by their appearance or characteristics	Without understanding the outcomes and being immersed in the duties
	Performs all the duties without any wishes or attachment from the results	Performs duties to fulfil the wishes with myth and arrogance	Ignores the prescribed duties, hurts others without any empathy
	Excited to perform all the duties	Likes to enjoy materialistic happiness,	Stubborn, cheat and insult others,

	without any arrogance or illusions	vulnerable to the dual facet outcomes, envious	lazy, depressed, wasting valuable time
Behaviour and Determination	Differentiate between Do's and Don'ts, fearfulness and fearlessness, and understand the importance of Moksha.	Unable to differentiate between righteous and heinous duties, Do’s and Don’ts	Manipulates and hallucinates between right and wrong, Do’s and Don’ts
	Unbreakable faith and self-controlled over the five physical elements, Mind and five universal elements	Ignoring the Eleven elements and attaching to the results	Fearful, depressed, hallucinations, dreaming due to Ignorance
The Journey	It feels challenging and time-consuming, but in the end, the results will feel like the Nectar.	It feels very easy, but as they go deep in, they face very difficult	Without self-realisation, permanently attached to laziness, lustful desires

Every individual performs their duties without any exception based on the above-referred characteristics. The Supreme Lord bifurcated such people into four groups. Brahmin, Warrior, Businessmen and Labour.

Brahmin	**Warrior**	**Businessmen**	**Labour**
Pleasantnes, control over the senses, cleanliness, patience, Truthfulnes, Knowledge of the Vedic sciences	Strong, Powerful, Determined, Brave, Fearlessness during warfare, Kindness and ruling-mindedness	Business, Trade, Protecting the Cows	Performing laborious duties / activities

People will perform the respective duties allocated to attain salvation. It is okay if people cannot fulfil their prescribed duties instead of fulfilling the duties prescribed for others.

A pleasant-minded person will reach the Supreme Soul with perfect behaviour, detached from likes and dislikes, controlling the senses and Mind, eating and speaking what is required, rising beyond pride and prestige, lust, and anger.

Such people are dear to HIM< are protected and will reach HIM in the end.

यदहङ्कारमाश्रित्य न योत्स्य इति मन्यसे ।
मिथ्यैष व्यवसायस्ते प्रकृतिस्त्वां नियोक्ष्यति ॥

Yad Ahankaaramaasritya Na Yotsya Iti Manyase
Mitheysha Vyvavasaayaste Prakrutistvaam Niyoksyati

Arjuna, even if you feel attached to the emotions and want to avoid the situation, you will still fight the battle naturally, being a warrior.

Krishna mentions that even if someone wants to avoid the situation and try to run away from their duties, as bifurcated humans as above and their characteristics, they will continue to perform their duties by nature.

ईश्वरः सर्वभूतानां हृद्देशेऽर्जुन तिष्ठति ।
भ्रामयन्सर्वभूतानि यन्त्रारूढानि मायया ॥

Eeswaraha Sarvabhootanaam Hrudyeshorjuna Tishtati
Bhraamayan Sarvabhootaani Yantraarudhaani Maayayaa

The Supreme Soul exists everywhere and controls everyone's paths. As mentioned, it is not just about living beings; the Supreme Lord controls the entire Universe, helping respective planets revolve in the prescribed orbits.

Krishna says I have told you the secret of the secrets. Absorb and understand entirely and decide what you want to do. Since you are my most beloved friend of mine, I have imbibed such divine knowledge.

मन्मना भव मद्भक्तो मद्याजी मां नमस्कुरु ।

मामेवैष्यसि सत्यं ते प्रतिजाने प्रियोऽसि मे ॥

Manmanaa Bhava Madbhaktho Madyaajee Maam Namaskuru

Maamevaishyasi Satyam Te Pratijaane Prayosi Me

If you comprehend me, be my devotee, pay respects, and follow the path that I have suggested, you will undoubtedly reach me. THIS IS MY PROMISE.

If we observe the above verse, Krishna is promising. The Supreme God is taking an oath to protect and help humankind, who performs their prescribed duties and devotes oneself to Krishna. Nothing else in this material world would be meaningful if HE were with us.

इदं ते नातपस्काय नाभक्ताय कदाचन।

न चाशुश्रूषवे वाच्यं न च मां योऽभ्यसूयति॥

Idam Te Naatapaskaaya Naa Bhaktaaya Kadaachana
Na Chaashusrushave Vaachayam Na Cha Maam Yobhyasuyati

These teachings must not be explained or taught to those who are ignorant, do not want to understand or hate HIM.

There is no point in explaining to those who are not ready to understand the essence of better ways of living and want to argue for the sake of argument. It is a sheer waste of energy. In my Mind, they live in the materialistic world and are struck in the vicious circle of life, ignoring the purpose of life.

य इमं परमं गुह्यं मद्भक्तेष्वभिधास्यति।
भक्तिं मयि परां कृत्वा मामेवैष्यत्यसंशयः।।

Ya Imam Param Guhyam Madbhakteshvabhidhaasyati
Bhaktim Mayi Paraam Krutvaa Maamevaishyasamshayaha

Those who spread this knowledge to his devotees with respect and dedication will undoubtedly attain unshakable trust and devotion and reach my abode. They are very dear to me.

I confirm that those who read this conversation with complete respect and devotion are considered to have performed intense penance with divine knowledge.

अर्जुन उवाच

नष्टो मोहः स्मृतिर्लब्धा त्वत्प्रसादान्मयाच्युत।

स्थितोऽस्मि गतसन्देहः करिष्ये वचनं तव।।

Arjuna Uvacha

Nashto Mohaha Smrutirlabhdhaa Tvatprasaadaanmayachyuta

Sthitosmi Gatasandehaha Karishey Vachanam Tava

Oh, Krishna, this conversation thoroughly washed away my illusions and confusion. I am now determined, confident, and ready to obey your instructions to fight the battle. I am ready to fight the greatest Mahabharata War.

सञ्जय उवाच

इत्यहं वासुदेवस्य पार्थस्य च महात्मनः।

संवादमिममश्रौषमद्भुतं रोमहर्षणम्।।

Sanjaya Uvacha

Ityaham Vaasudevasya Paarthasya Cha Mahaatmanaha

Samvaadamimamamsroshamadbhutam Romaharshanam

Sanjaya says, "I am getting goosebumps after listening to such a brilliant and divine conversation between Krishna and Arjuna. Witnessing the indescribable universal form of Sri Krishna gives me eternal happiness."

यत्र योगेश्वरः कृष्णो यत्र पार्थो धनुर्धरः।

तत्र श्रीर्विजयो भूतिर्ध्रुवा नीतिर्मतिर्मम।।

Yatra Yogeswaraha Krishno Yatra Paartho Dhanurtharaha

Tatra Sreervijayo Bhootirdhruvaa Neetirmatirmama

It is guaranteed that wherever The Supreme Yogi (Lord Sri Krishna) and the greatest warrior, Arjuna, with his mighty Bow, reside, that place is filled with Wealth, Victory, Power and Truthfulness.

In summary, the complete conversation initiated from an emotional trauma of personal loss of near and dear due to the war, Arjuna evolved to understand the true purpose of life.

Sri Krishna did not tell Arjuna to pick up the Gandivam (the mighty Bow) and kill his opposition to win the war and possess a piece of land. Do we find ourselves on a battlefield and fight against enemies with weapons?

Think about this: The true battle is within human beings. A fight between right and wrong. Overcoming evil-mindedness, greed, cheating, hurting others, and disrupting their peace is essential for building a strong, positive character. It is all about embracing live-and-let-live philosophy.

Every living being needs to perform their duties. As long as those duties are performed without greediness and selfishness will keep humankind away from committing sinful acts.

When we treat everyone equally, this world has no enemy or enmity. Even if someone wants to hurt you, as Krishna said, maintain Silence (मौनं चैवास्मि गुह्यानां – I am the Silence in the Secrets). As they continue to hurt you, they are hurting the Supreme Lord in you in the form of supreme Soul. The Supreme Lord resides everywhere, even in the person who is hurting you. In other words, they are hurting themselves. Now, think about it: do you want to hurt yourself? Please give it a thought.

Bhagavad Gita is not a book for retired people. It teaches lessons about how to conduct oneself in daily life. Unfortunately, in some instances, Bhagavat Gita is played during a person's last journey primarily because of the first two chapters which focused on the Arjuna's grief and Krishna's affirmation about rebirth, overshadowed the broader principles of the Bhagavat Gita.

However, a thorough study of the entire Bhagavat Gita reveals that it encompasses much more than just death and rebirth. It offers profound philosophy and knowledge on ways of living, communication, management and leadership skills and understanding the difference between the right and the wrong and many more.

In my opinion, the Supreme God gives multiple opportunities for humankind to fine-tune and evolve as reverent individuals to reach HIS supreme abode forever. It is not possible to get HIM in one life. Hence, the Sanatana Dharma strongly advocates the concept of rebirth and confirms that a soul continues to travel from one physical body to the other.

Throughout the teaching, Krishna spoke about ways of living, building a strong character with a pure soul by offering sacrifices (Yagna), Donations (Dana), and Penance (Tapa).

He also described well-being practices such as meditation, healthy eating habits, and how to forgive and help people.

Therefore, Sanatana Dharma is not just related to the Hindu religion or religious text but a way of life.

How a student respect teachers (consider Arjuna as an example, how a mighty warrior respected his gurus, Krishna as Jagatguru (The teacher of the universe), how younger generation respect elders. It teaches you to stay strong in difficult times. If the Supreme Power is with you, nothing can go wrong.

As Krishna repeatedly stated, finding such pure and soulful people is rare—one in millions. There is always a possibility for the humankind to try to be that one person to live meaningful lives with Dharma, treating everyone equally, and helping people in need.

With that, the Yagna of documenting the greatest teachings ever as my first book comes to an end and the journey in search of Sri Krishna begins.

Krishnam Vande Jagadgurum

Om Namo Bhagavate Vasudevaya,